PENTEST+ EXAM PASS (PT0-002)

PENETRATION TESTING AND VULNERABILITY MANAGEMENT FOR CYBERSECURITY PROFESSIONALS

4 BOOKS IN 1

BOOK 1
PENTEST+ EXAM PASS: FOUNDATION FUNDAMENTALS

BOOK 2
PENTEST+ EXAM PASS: ADVANCED TECHNIQUES AND TOOLS

BOOK 3
PENTEST+ EXAM PASS: NETWORK EXPLOITATION AND DEFENSE STRATEGIES

BOOK 4
PENTEST+ EXAM PASS: EXPERT INSIGHTS AND REAL-WORLD SCENARIOS

ROB BOTWRIGHT

Published by Rob Botwright
Library of Congress Cataloging-in-Publication Data
ISBN 978-1-83938-788-3
Cover design by Rizzo

Disclaimer

The contents of this book are based on extensive research and the best available historical sources. However, the author and publisher make no claims, promises, or guarantees about the accuracy, completeness, or adequacy of the information contained herein. The information in this book is provided on an "as is" basis, and the author and publisher disclaim any and all liability for any errors, omissions, or inaccuracies in the information or for any actions taken in reliance on such information. The opinions and views expressed in this book are those of the author and do not necessarily reflect the official policy or position of any organization or individual mentioned in this book. Any reference to specific people, places, or events is intended only to provide historical context and is not intended to defame or malign any group, individual, or entity. The information in this book is intended for educational and entertainment purposes only. It is not intended to be a substitute for professional advice or judgment. Readers are encouraged to conduct their own research and to seek professional advice where appropriate. Every effort has been made to obtain necessary permissions and acknowledgments for all images and other copyrighted material used in this book. Any errors or omissions in this regard are unintentional, and the author and publisher will correct them in future editions.

BOOK 1 - PENTEST+ EXAM PASS: FOUNDATION FUNDAMENTALS

BOOK 2 - PENTEST+ EXAM PASS: ADVANCED TECHNIQUES AND TOOLS

BOOK 3 - PENTEST+ EXAM PASS: NETWORK EXPLOITATION AND DEFENSE STRATEGIES

BOOK 4 - PENTEST+ EXAM PASS: EXPERT INSIGHTS AND REAL-WORLD SCENARIOS

Introduction

Welcome to the "PENTEST+ EXAM PASS: (PT0-002)" book bundle, a comprehensive resource designed to help cybersecurity professionals prepare for the CompTIA PenTest+ certification exam. This bundle consists of four distinct books, each focused on different aspects of penetration testing and vulnerability management.

Book 1, "PENTEST+ EXAM PASS: FOUNDATION FUNDAMENTALS," serves as the starting point for your journey towards becoming a certified penetration tester. It covers the foundational concepts and methodologies essential for understanding penetration testing, vulnerability assessment, and risk management.

In Book 2, "PENTEST+ EXAM PASS: ADVANCED TECHNIQUES AND TOOLS," we dive deeper into advanced techniques and tools used by cybersecurity professionals to identify, exploit, and mitigate vulnerabilities in complex environments. This book equips you with practical skills and knowledge to tackle sophisticated cyber threats effectively.

Moving forward, Book 3, "PENTEST+ EXAM PASS: NETWORK EXPLOITATION AND DEFENSE STRATEGIES," focuses on network exploitation and defense strategies. It provides insights into the intricacies of network security and how attackers exploit vulnerabilities to compromise systems. Additionally, it offers valuable guidance on implementing defensive measures to protect against such attacks.

Finally, Book 4, "PENTEST+ EXAM PASS: EXPERT INSIGHTS AND REAL-WORLD SCENARIOS," goes beyond the exam syllabus, offering expert insights and real-world scenarios to deepen your understanding of penetration testing and vulnerability management. Through case studies and practical examples, you will gain valuable insights into the challenges and complexities of real-world cybersecurity scenarios.

Whether you are new to penetration testing or a seasoned professional looking to enhance your skills, the "PENTEST+ EXAM PASS: (PT0-002)" book bundle provides a comprehensive and practical resource to help you succeed in the dynamic and challenging field of cybersecurity. Let's embark on this journey together and prepare to ace the CompTIA PenTest+ exam!

BOOK 1
PENTEST+ EXAM PASS
FOUNDATION FUNDAMENTALS

ROB BOTWRIGHT

Chapter 1: Introduction to Penetration Testing

Penetration testing and vulnerability assessment are two crucial components of a comprehensive cybersecurity strategy. While both aim to enhance the security posture of an organization, they serve distinct purposes and employ different methodologies. Penetration testing, often referred to as ethical hacking, simulates real-world attacks to identify and exploit vulnerabilities in systems, applications, and networks. This proactive approach helps organizations understand their security weaknesses and potential impact if exploited by malicious actors. In contrast, vulnerability assessment focuses on identifying, classifying, and prioritizing vulnerabilities within an IT infrastructure. It provides a snapshot of the organization's security posture at a given moment and helps in remediation efforts. Penetration testing goes beyond vulnerability assessment by actively exploiting identified vulnerabilities to assess the effectiveness of existing security controls. It simulates the tactics, techniques, and procedures (TTPs) of attackers to uncover hidden vulnerabilities and weaknesses that may not be detected through automated scans alone. A penetration test typically follows a predefined scope and methodology, which may include reconnaissance, vulnerability scanning, exploitation, post-exploitation, and reporting. During reconnaissance, penetration testers gather information about the target environment, such as network topology, systems, and services. This may involve using tools like Nmap, Netcat, or Recon-ng to discover hosts, open ports, and running services. Once reconnaissance is complete, vulnerability scanning tools like Nessus, OpenVAS, or Nikto are used to identify known vulnerabilities and misconfigurations. These tools automate the process of identifying common security issues, such as missing patches, default credentials, and insecure configurations. After identifying potential vulnerabilities, penetration testers attempt to exploit them to gain unauthorized access to systems or data. This phase involves using various exploitation techniques, including buffer overflow attacks, SQL injection, cross-site scripting (XSS), and privilege escalation. Tools like Metasploit, Exploit-DB, and SQLMap are commonly used to launch these attacks. However, it's essential to note that penetration testing should always be conducted with the organization's explicit permission and within a controlled environment to minimize the risk of disruption or damage. Once access is gained, penetration testers perform post-exploitation activities to assess the extent of the compromise and the ability to maintain access. This may involve escalating privileges, pivoting to other systems, or exfiltrating sensitive data. Throughout the penetration testing process, detailed documentation is essential to capture findings, including exploited vulnerabilities, compromised systems, and recommended remediation actions. This documentation is compiled into a comprehensive report, which outlines the test objectives, methodologies, findings, and recommendations for improving security posture. In contrast, vulnerability assessment focuses on identifying and prioritizing vulnerabilities based on their severity, impact, and likelihood of exploitation. Vulnerability scanners generate reports that list detected vulnerabilities along with their associated risks and recommendations for remediation. While vulnerability assessment provides valuable insights into the organization's security posture, it does not validate the exploitability of identified vulnerabilities or assess the effectiveness of existing security controls. Therefore, penetration testing is often recommended in addition to vulnerability assessment to provide a more thorough evaluation of security defenses. Additionally, penetration testing helps organizations comply with regulatory requirements and industry standards, such as PCI DSS, HIPAA, and ISO 27001, which mandate regular security testing and risk assessments. By proactively identifying and addressing security weaknesses, organizations can reduce the likelihood of successful cyber attacks and minimize the potential impact of security breaches. In summary, while both penetration testing and vulnerability assessment are essential components of a robust cybersecurity program, they serve distinct purposes and employ different methodologies. Penetration testing simulates real-world attacks to identify and exploit vulnerabilities actively, while vulnerability assessment focuses on identifying and prioritizing vulnerabilities within an IT infrastructure. By combining both approaches, organizations can achieve a more comprehensive understanding of their security posture and implement effective risk mitigation strategies.

Penetration testing plays a critical role in modern cybersecurity strategies, serving as a proactive measure to identify and address vulnerabilities before they can be exploited by malicious actors. By simulating real-world attacks, penetration testing helps organizations assess the effectiveness of their security defenses and prioritize remediation efforts. One of the primary reasons for the importance of penetration testing is its ability to uncover hidden security weaknesses that may not be apparent through automated scans or vulnerability assessments alone. Unlike automated tools, which can only identify known vulnerabilities and misconfigurations, penetration testers can think and act like attackers, leveraging their creativity and expertise to identify novel attack vectors. This human-centric approach enables penetration testers to uncover vulnerabilities that automated tools may overlook, such as logic flaws, business logic vulnerabilities, and insider threats. Moreover, penetration testing provides organizations with actionable insights into their security posture, allowing them to make informed decisions about risk management and resource allocation. By identifying and prioritizing vulnerabilities based on their severity, impact, and likelihood of exploitation, organizations can focus their efforts on mitigating the most critical security risks first. This risk-based approach helps organizations allocate limited resources effectively and maximize the impact of their cybersecurity investments. Additionally, penetration testing helps organizations comply with regulatory requirements and industry standards, which mandate regular security testing and risk assessments. For example, regulations such as the Payment Card Industry Data Security Standard (PCI DSS), Health Insurance Portability and Accountability Act (HIPAA), and General Data Protection Regulation (GDPR) require organizations to conduct regular security testing to protect sensitive data and ensure compliance with legal and regulatory requirements. By conducting penetration tests, organizations can demonstrate their commitment to cybersecurity and mitigate the risk of non-compliance penalties and reputational damage. Furthermore, penetration testing helps organizations build trust and confidence with customers, partners, and stakeholders by demonstrating their commitment to protecting sensitive information and maintaining a secure operating environment. By proactively identifying and addressing security weaknesses, organizations can enhance their reputation and differentiate themselves from competitors who neglect cybersecurity. Moreover, penetration testing helps organizations validate the effectiveness of their security controls and incident response capabilities. By simulating real-world attacks, penetration testers can assess how well security defenses detect, prevent, and respond to security incidents. This allows organizations to identify gaps in their security posture and refine their security policies, procedures, and incident response plans accordingly. Additionally, penetration testing helps organizations evaluate the security of third-party vendors and suppliers who have access to their systems or data. By conducting regular security assessments of third-party vendors, organizations can ensure that they meet minimum security requirements and comply with contractual obligations. This helps mitigate the risk of supply chain attacks and data breaches resulting from vulnerabilities in third-party systems or services. Moreover, penetration testing helps organizations stay ahead of emerging threats and evolving attack techniques by simulating the tactics, techniques, and procedures (TTPs) of real-world attackers. By continuously testing and refining their security defenses, organizations can adapt to changing threat landscapes and improve their ability to detect and respond to emerging threats. In summary, penetration testing plays a crucial role in modern cybersecurity strategies, helping organizations identify and address vulnerabilities before they can be exploited by malicious actors. By simulating real-world attacks, penetration testing provides organizations with actionable insights into their security posture, helps them comply with regulatory requirements, builds trust with customers and stakeholders, validates security controls and incident response capabilities, evaluates third-party vendors, and stays ahead of emerging threats.

Chapter 2: Understanding Cybersecurity Fundamentals

The CIA Triad, consisting of Confidentiality, Integrity, and Availability, serves as a foundational framework for designing and evaluating information security controls in organizations. Confidentiality refers to the protection of sensitive information from unauthorized access or disclosure, ensuring that only authorized individuals or entities can access or view the data. This is achieved through encryption, access controls, and data classification policies, which restrict access to sensitive information based on the principle of least privilege. For example, organizations can use encryption algorithms such as AES (Advanced Encryption Standard) or RSA (Rivest-Shamir-Adleman) to encrypt data at rest and in transit, ensuring that even if an attacker gains unauthorized access to the data, they cannot read or decipher its contents without the encryption key. Access controls, such as role-based access control (RBAC) or attribute-based access control (ABAC), help enforce the principle of least privilege by granting users access to only the resources and data they need to perform their job duties. Data classification policies classify data based on its sensitivity level, allowing organizations to apply appropriate security controls based on the data's classification. Integrity, the second pillar of the CIA Triad, ensures that data remains accurate, complete, and unaltered during storage, transmission, and processing. This is essential for maintaining the trustworthiness and reliability of data, as any unauthorized or unintended modifications can lead to data corruption, loss of credibility, and potential financial or legal consequences. To ensure data integrity, organizations use cryptographic hash functions such as SHA-256 (Secure Hash Algorithm 256-bit) to generate checksums or hashes of data, which can be compared before and after transmission to verify its integrity. For example, organizations can use the md5sum command in Linux or the CertUtil -hashfile command in Windows to calculate the MD5 hash of a file and verify its integrity by comparing it with the original hash. Additionally, digital signatures and digital certificates are used to verify the authenticity and integrity of data and messages, ensuring that they have not been tampered with or altered by unauthorized parties. Availability, the third pillar of the CIA Triad, ensures that information and resources are accessible and usable when needed by authorized users. This involves implementing redundancy, fault tolerance, and disaster recovery measures to minimize downtime and ensure business continuity in the event of hardware failures, natural disasters, or cyber attacks. Redundancy involves duplicating critical systems, components, or resources to ensure that if one fails, another can take its place seamlessly, minimizing disruption to operations. For example, organizations can use RAID (Redundant Array of Independent Disks) to create redundant storage arrays that distribute data across multiple disks, ensuring that if one disk fails, data can still be accessed from the remaining disks. Fault tolerance involves designing systems and architectures that can continue to function even in the presence of faults or failures, such as redundant power supplies, network links, or servers. Disaster recovery involves developing and implementing plans and procedures to recover data, systems, and operations in the event of a catastrophic event or outage. This may involve regularly backing up data to off-site locations, maintaining standby or hot spare systems, and testing recovery procedures to ensure they are effective and reliable. In summary, the CIA Triad provides a comprehensive framework for designing, implementing, and evaluating information security controls to protect the confidentiality, integrity, and availability of data and resources. By addressing these three pillars, organizations can establish a strong security posture that mitigates risks, safeguards sensitive information, and ensures the reliability and availability of critical systems and services.

Principles of Defense in Depth are fundamental to modern cybersecurity strategies, providing a layered approach to protect information systems from a wide range of threats and vulnerabilities. This approach recognizes that no single security measure is sufficient to defend against all potential attacks and emphasizes the need for multiple layers of defense to mitigate risks effectively. The concept of Defense in Depth is based on the idea of building multiple layers of security controls, each serving as a barrier to prevent or deter attackers from compromising sensitive data or systems. These layers of defense work together to create overlapping and mutually reinforcing protections, making it more difficult for attackers to penetrate the organization's defenses and achieve their objectives. The first principle of Defense in Depth is to establish a robust perimeter defense to protect the organization's network from external threats. This involves deploying firewalls, intrusion detection/prevention systems (IDS/IPS), and secure gateways to monitor and control traffic entering and leaving the network. For example, organizations can use the iptables command in Linux to configure a firewall to filter incoming and outgoing traffic based on predefined rules. Additionally, network segmentation and access controls can be implemented to restrict access to sensitive resources and limit the lateral movement of attackers within the network. The second principle of Defense in Depth is to secure the internal network by implementing controls to prevent and detect unauthorized access and activities. This includes deploying network access control (NAC) solutions, endpoint protection software, and security information and event management (SIEM) systems to monitor and respond to security events in real-time. For example, organizations can use the nmap command to scan their internal network for open ports and running services, allowing them to identify potential security vulnerabilities and misconfigurations. Additionally, user authentication and authorization mechanisms, such as multi-factor authentication (MFA) and role-based access control (RBAC), can be implemented to ensure that only authorized users have access to sensitive resources and data. The third principle of Defense in Depth is to protect data at rest and in transit by implementing encryption and data loss prevention (DLP) solutions. Encryption ensures that data remains confidential and secure, even if it is intercepted or accessed by unauthorized parties. For example, organizations can use the openssl command in Linux to encrypt files using symmetric or asymmetric encryption algorithms such as AES or RSA. Additionally, DLP solutions can be deployed to monitor and control the movement of sensitive data within the organization's network, preventing unauthorized access or exfiltration. The fourth principle of Defense in Depth is to establish strong authentication and identity management controls to verify the identity of users and devices accessing the organization's systems and resources. This includes implementing strong password policies, user account management procedures, and biometric authentication mechanisms to prevent unauthorized access and protect against identity theft and credential-based attacks. For example, organizations can use the passwd command in Linux to change a user's password or the pam_tally2 command to monitor failed login attempts and lock user accounts after a certain number of retries. Additionally, organizations can deploy identity and access management (IAM) solutions to centralize user authentication and authorization processes and enforce consistent security policies across the organization. The fifth principle of Defense in Depth is to continuously monitor and assess the organization's security posture to identify and respond to emerging threats and vulnerabilities. This involves deploying security monitoring tools, such as intrusion detection systems (IDS), security information and event management (SIEM) systems, and endpoint detection and response (EDR) solutions, to collect and analyze security-related data and events. For example, organizations can use the tcpdump command in Linux to capture network traffic for analysis or the snort command to detect and alert on suspicious network activity. Additionally, regular security assessments, such as vulnerability scanning and penetration testing, can be conducted to identify and remediate security weaknesses before they can be exploited by attackers. In summary, Principles of Defense in Depth provide a comprehensive framework for building resilient and effective cybersecurity defenses. By implementing multiple layers of security controls, organizations can reduce the likelihood and impact of security breaches, protect sensitive data and resources, and maintain the integrity and availability of their systems and services.

Chapter 3: Exploring Penetration Testing Methodologies

Comparison of penetration testing frameworks is essential for security professionals to choose the most suitable tool for their specific requirements and objectives. Penetration testing frameworks provide a structured approach to conducting security assessments and identifying vulnerabilities in information systems. Each framework offers unique features, capabilities, and methodologies, making it important to evaluate them based on factors such as ease of use, flexibility, coverage of attack techniques, and community support. One of the most widely used penetration testing frameworks is Metasploit, an open-source platform that provides a comprehensive set of tools for penetration testing, exploit development, and vulnerability research. Metasploit offers a user-friendly interface and a vast library of pre-built exploits and payloads, making it ideal for both beginners and experienced penetration testers. The msfconsole command is used to launch the Metasploit framework, allowing users to interact with various modules and execute exploits against target systems. Another popular penetration testing framework is Burp Suite, a web application security testing tool that is widely used by security professionals to identify and exploit vulnerabilities in web applications. Burp Suite offers a suite of tools for web application scanning, crawling, and exploitation, including a proxy, scanner, intruder, repeater, and sequencer. The burpsuite command is used to launch the Burp Suite application, allowing users to configure and customize their testing workflows. In addition to Metasploit and Burp Suite, there are several other penetration testing frameworks available, each with its own strengths and weaknesses. For example, Nmap is a powerful network scanning tool that is widely used for reconnaissance and discovery during penetration tests. The nmap command is used to launch Nmap, allowing users to scan target networks and hosts for open ports, services, and vulnerabilities. Similarly, SQLMap is a popular tool for detecting and exploiting SQL injection vulnerabilities in web applications. The sqlmap command is used to launch SQLMap, allowing users to automate the process of identifying and exploiting SQL injection vulnerabilities in target web applications. Other notable penetration testing frameworks include Wireshark, a network protocol analyzer; Hydra, a password cracking tool; and Aircrack-ng, a suite of tools for testing wireless network security. Each of these frameworks offers unique features and capabilities, making them suitable for different types of security assessments and objectives. For example, Wireshark is commonly used for analyzing network traffic and identifying suspicious or malicious activity, while Hydra is often used for brute-force attacks against password-protected services. Aircrack-ng, on the other hand, is specifically designed for testing and securing wireless networks, making it ideal for penetration testers conducting wireless security assessments. When comparing penetration testing frameworks, it's important to consider factors such as ease of use, documentation, community support, and compatibility with existing tools and workflows. Additionally, organizations should evaluate the cost and licensing requirements of each framework to ensure that it aligns with their budget and compliance requirements. By carefully evaluating and selecting the right penetration testing framework, security professionals can effectively identify and mitigate security vulnerabilities in their organization's information systems, helping to protect against cyber attacks and data breaches. The penetration testing process is a systematic approach to identifying and exploiting vulnerabilities in information systems, networks, and applications to assess their security posture and effectiveness. The process typically consists of several distinct phases, each with its own objectives, methodologies, and techniques. The first phase of the penetration testing process is reconnaissance, also known as information gathering or footprinting, which involves gathering information about the target organization, its systems, and its infrastructure. This phase aims to identify potential attack vectors and entry points that can be exploited during the penetration test. Tools such as Nmap, Recon-ng, and Shodan can be used to perform reconnaissance activities, including network scanning, domain enumeration, and OSINT (Open-Source Intelligence) gathering. Once reconnaissance is complete, the next phase is scanning, which involves identifying and mapping out the target's network topology, services, and vulnerabilities. This phase aims to identify potential security weaknesses that can be exploited to gain unauthorized access to the target's systems or data. Tools such as Nessus, OpenVAS, and Nikto can be used to perform vulnerability scanning and identify common security issues such as missing patches, misconfigurations, and insecure services. After scanning, the penetration tester moves on to the exploitation phase, where they attempt to exploit identified vulnerabilities to gain unauthorized access to the target's systems or data. This phase involves using various techniques and tools to launch exploits against vulnerable services or applications, such as Metasploit, Exploit-DB, and SQLMap. It is important for penetration testers to exercise caution and obtain explicit authorization from the target organization before attempting to exploit vulnerabilities, as unauthorized exploitation can lead to legal and ethical issues. Once access has been gained, the penetration tester proceeds to the post-exploitation phase, where they attempt to escalate privileges, establish persistence, and exfiltrate sensitive data from the target's systems. This phase aims to simulate the tactics, techniques, and procedures (TTPs) of real-world attackers and assess the target's ability to detect and respond to security incidents. Tools such as Mimikatz, PowerSploit, and BloodHound can be used to perform post-exploitation activities, including privilege escalation, lateral movement, and data exfiltration. Throughout the penetration testing process, the penetration tester maintains detailed documentation of their activities, findings, and recommendations. This documentation is compiled into a comprehensive report, which outlines the objectives of the penetration test, the methodologies used, the vulnerabilities identified, and the recommended remediation actions. The final phase of the penetration testing process is reporting, where the penetration tester presents their findings and recommendations to the target organization's stakeholders, including IT staff, management, and executives. The penetration test report should be clear, concise, and actionable, providing the target organization with the information they need to improve their security posture and mitigate identified vulnerabilities. In addition to presenting the findings and recommendations, the penetration tester may also provide guidance and support to the target organization's IT staff on implementing remediation actions and improving their security practices. Overall, the penetration testing process is a vital component of a comprehensive cybersecurity program, helping organizations identify and mitigate security risks, protect sensitive data, and enhance their overall security posture. By following a systematic approach to penetration testing and adhering to best practices and ethical guidelines, organizations can effectively assess their security defenses and minimize the risk of cyber attacks and data breaches.

Chapter 4: Basics of Network Reconnaissance

Passive and active reconnaissance techniques are essential components of the information gathering phase in penetration testing and cybersecurity assessments, each offering distinct advantages and challenges in discovering information about target systems and networks. Passive reconnaissance involves collecting information about the target without directly interacting with it, minimizing the risk of detection and disruption. This can include gathering publicly available information from sources such as search engines, social media platforms, public records, and WHOIS databases. Passive reconnaissance techniques aim to gather information discreetly, without alerting the target organization to the fact that they are being surveilled. Tools such as Maltego, Shodan, and theHarvester can be used to perform passive reconnaissance activities, including domain enumeration, email harvesting, and network footprinting. For example, theMaltego command is used to launch the Maltego application, allowing users to perform OSINT (Open-Source Intelligence) gathering and visualize relationships between entities such as domains, IP addresses, and email addresses. Active reconnaissance, on the other hand, involves actively probing and interacting with the target's systems and networks to gather information. While active reconnaissance can provide more detailed and accurate information about the target, it also carries a higher risk of detection and potential disruption. Active reconnaissance techniques include network scanning, port scanning, and vulnerability scanning, which involve sending packets to the target's systems and analyzing their responses to identify potential vulnerabilities and weaknesses. Tools such as Nmap, Nessus, and OpenVAS can be used to perform active reconnaissance activities, including host discovery, port scanning, and vulnerability assessment. For example, theNmap command is used to launch the Nmap application, allowing users to perform network scans to identify open ports, running services, and potential security vulnerabilities. While passive reconnaissance techniques are less intrusive and may be less likely to trigger security alerts, they are also limited in their ability to gather detailed information about the target. Passive reconnaissance relies on publicly available information and may not provide insight into internal systems or network configurations. Active reconnaissance, on the other hand, provides a more comprehensive view of the target's systems and networks but carries a higher risk of detection and potential legal and ethical implications. When conducting penetration tests or cybersecurity assessments, it is essential to carefully consider the advantages and limitations of both passive and active reconnaissance techniques and to use them in combination to gather the most accurate and actionable information about the target. By combining passive and active reconnaissance techniques, penetration testers can gain a more comprehensive understanding of the target's systems and networks and identify potential security vulnerabilities and weaknesses more effectively. Additionally, it is important to obtain explicit authorization from the target organization before conducting active reconnaissance activities to ensure compliance with legal and ethical guidelines. Overall, passive and active reconnaissance techniques are essential tools in the arsenal of penetration testers and cybersecurity professionals, providing valuable insights into the security posture of target systems and networks and helping to identify and mitigate potential security risks.

Using Open Source Intelligence (OSINT) in reconnaissance is a crucial aspect of cybersecurity and intelligence gathering, providing valuable insights into potential threats, vulnerabilities, and adversaries. OSINT refers to the collection and analysis of information from publicly available sources, including websites, social media platforms, online forums, public records, and government publications. OSINT is often used by cybersecurity professionals, law enforcement agencies, and intelligence analysts to gather information about individuals, organizations, and events to support decision-making and investigations. One of the key benefits of OSINT is its accessibility, as many of the sources used for OSINT are freely available on the internet and do not require specialized tools or expertise to access. However, while OSINT provides a wealth of information, it also presents challenges in terms of volume, accuracy, and relevance, requiring analysts to carefully evaluate and verify the information they collect. OSINT can be used in reconnaissance to gather information about potential targets, such as organizations, individuals, or specific assets, to assess their security posture and identify potential vulnerabilities. This can include gathering information about the target's infrastructure, employees, partners, suppliers, and customers, as well as their online presence and activities. OSINT techniques can include web scraping, social media monitoring, search engine queries, and data analysis, which can be performed using a variety of tools and techniques. For example, the OSINT framework is a popular tool for conducting OSINT investigations, providing a collection of open-source intelligence tools and resources for gathering and analyzing information from various online sources. The osintframework command is used to launch the OSINT framework, allowing users to access its collection of tools and resources for OSINT investigations. Another popular OSINT tool is Maltego, which provides a graphical interface for visualizing and analyzing relationships between entities such as domains, IP addresses, email addresses, and social media profiles. The maltego command is used to launch the Maltego application, allowing users to perform OSINT investigations and gather information about potential targets. OSINT can also be used to gather information about potential threats and adversaries, such as cybercriminals, hacktivists, and nation-state actors, to assess their capabilities, motivations, and intentions. This can include monitoring online forums, social media platforms, and dark web marketplaces for discussions, announcements, and activities related to cyber attacks, data breaches, and other malicious activities. OSINT techniques can be used to identify indicators of compromise (IOCs), such as IP addresses, domain names, email addresses, and file hashes associated with known threats, which can be used to enhance threat intelligence and support incident response efforts. Additionally, OSINT can be used to gather information about emerging threats and trends in the cybersecurity landscape, such as new vulnerabilities, attack techniques, and malware variants, to proactively identify and mitigate potential risks. By monitoring online sources for information about security advisories, data breaches, and other cybersecurity events, organizations can stay informed about the latest threats and take proactive measures to protect their systems and data. However, while OSINT provides valuable insights into potential threats and vulnerabilities, it also presents challenges in terms of volume, accuracy, and relevance. The sheer volume of information available through OSINT sources can be overwhelming, requiring analysts to filter and prioritize information based on its importance and relevance to their objectives. Additionally, the accuracy of information obtained through OSINT sources can vary widely, requiring analysts to verify and corroborate information from multiple sources to ensure its reliability. Furthermore, not all information obtained through OSINT sources may be relevant or actionable, requiring analysts to carefully evaluate and interpret the information they collect in the context of their specific objectives and requirements. Despite these challenges, OSINT remains a valuable tool in the arsenal of cybersecurity professionals and intelligence analysts, providing valuable insights into potential threats, vulnerabilities, and adversaries. By leveraging OSINT techniques and tools, organizations can gather information from publicly available sources to support decision-making, investigations, and incident response efforts, helping to enhance their security posture and protect against emerging threats.

Chapter 5: Essential Tools for Penetration Testing

Kali Linux is a powerful and versatile Linux distribution designed for penetration testing, digital forensics, and security research, providing a wide range of tools and utilities for cybersecurity professionals and enthusiasts. Developed and maintained by Offensive Security, Kali Linux is based on Debian and is specifically tailored to meet the needs of security professionals who require a robust and comprehensive platform for conducting security assessments and investigations. One of the key features of Kali Linux is its extensive collection of pre-installed tools and utilities, which include penetration testing tools, network analysis tools, forensics tools, reverse engineering tools, and wireless hacking tools. These tools are organized into categories and can be accessed through the Kali Linux menu system or launched from the command line. For example, the nmap command is used to launch the Nmap network scanning tool, allowing users to perform port scans, host discovery, and service enumeration on target networks. Additionally, the metasploit command is used to launch the Metasploit Framework, a powerful penetration testing tool that provides a wide range of exploits, payloads, and auxiliary modules for testing the security of target systems. Kali Linux also includes a number of specialized tools for conducting wireless network assessments, such as Aircrack-ng, Reaver, and Wireshark, which can be used to crack WEP and WPA/WPA2 encryption, capture and analyze network traffic, and perform packet injection attacks. In addition to its pre-installed tools, Kali Linux supports a wide range of hardware platforms and architectures, including 32-bit and 64-bit x86 systems, ARM-based devices, and virtualization platforms such as VMware and VirtualBox. This flexibility allows users to run Kali Linux on a variety of hardware devices, including desktop computers, laptops, servers, and embedded systems, making it suitable for a wide range of security testing scenarios. Kali Linux also provides a number of features and utilities to support penetration testing and security research, such as the ability to create custom ISO images, encrypt and password-protect sensitive data, and configure network interfaces and firewall rules. For example, the gpg command is used to encrypt and decrypt files using GPG (GNU Privacy Guard), allowing users to protect sensitive data from unauthorized access. Additionally, the ifconfig command is used to configure network interfaces, set IP addresses, and enable/disable network connections, while the iptables command is used to configure firewall rules and packet filtering policies. Another key feature of Kali Linux is its focus on security and privacy, with built-in support for full-disk encryption, anonymous browsing, and secure communication protocols. For example, Kali Linux includes the Tor Browser, a web browser that routes internet traffic through the Tor network to anonymize users' IP addresses and protect their online privacy. Additionally, Kali Linux includes tools for encrypting email communications, such as GnuPG and Enigmail, which can be used to send and receive encrypted messages securely. Overall, Kali Linux is a versatile and powerful platform for penetration testing, digital forensics, and security research, providing a wide range of tools and utilities for cybersecurity professionals and enthusiasts. Whether you're conducting security assessments, investigating security incidents, or learning about cybersecurity, Kali Linux provides the tools and resources you need to get the job done. Popular penetration testing tools play a critical role in the arsenal of cybersecurity professionals, providing them with the capabilities needed to identify and exploit vulnerabilities in target systems and networks, among other tasks. One of the most widely used penetration testing tools is Nmap, a powerful network scanning tool that allows users to discover hosts and services on a network, as well as identify open ports, running services, and potential security vulnerabilities. The nmap command is used to launch Nmap and initiate scans, while various options and flags can be used to customize the scan parameters and output format. Another popular penetration testing tool is Metasploit, an open-source framework that provides a wide range of exploits, payloads, and auxiliary modules for penetration testing and exploitation. The msfconsole command is used to launch the Metasploit framework, allowing users to interact with various modules and execute exploits against target systems. Metasploit also includes a web-based interface called Armitage, which provides a graphical interface for managing targets, exploits, and sessions. Wireshark is another popular penetration testing tool that allows users to capture and analyze network traffic in real-time, enabling them to identify security vulnerabilities, troubleshoot network issues, and detect malicious activity. The wireshark command is used to launch Wireshark and start capturing packets on a network interface, while various filters and display options can be used to analyze specific protocols, conversations, or packets of interest. Burp Suite is a comprehensive web application security testing tool that allows users to perform various tasks such as scanning for vulnerabilities, intercepting and modifying HTTP requests, and testing for common security issues such as SQL injection and cross-site scripting (XSS). The burpsuite command is used to launch Burp Suite and access its various tools and features, including the Proxy, Scanner, Intruder, Repeater, and Sequencer. Hydra is a popular password cracking tool that allows users to perform brute-force attacks against password-protected services and applications. The hydra command is used to launch Hydra and specify the target service, username list, password list, and other options required for the brute-force attack. John the Ripper is another password cracking tool that supports various password cracking techniques, including dictionary attacks, brute-force attacks, and rainbow table attacks. The john command is used to launch John the Ripper and specify the target password file, wordlist, and cracking mode. Aircrack-ng is a suite of tools for testing and securing wireless networks, including tools for capturing and analyzing wireless packets, cracking WEP and WPA/WPA2 encryption, and performing deauthentication and packet injection attacks. The airodump-ng command is used to capture wireless packets on a network interface, while the aireplay-ng command is used to perform deauthentication and packet injection attacks. Nessus is a popular vulnerability scanning tool that allows users to scan target systems and networks for known vulnerabilities and misconfigurations, providing detailed reports and remediation recommendations. The nessus command is used to launch Nessus and initiate scans, while various options and settings can be configured to customize the scan parameters and reporting format. OpenVAS is an open-source vulnerability scanning tool that is similar to Nessus, providing users with the ability to scan target systems and networks for known vulnerabilities and misconfigurations. The openvas command is used to launch OpenVAS and access its various scanning and reporting features. Nikto is a web server vulnerability scanner that allows users to scan web servers for common security issues such as outdated software, misconfigurations, and known vulnerabilities. The nikto command is used to launch Nikto and specify the target web server, port, and other scan parameters. Sqlmap is a popular tool for detecting and exploiting SQL injection vulnerabilities in web applications, allowing users to automate the process of identifying and exploiting SQL injection flaws. The sqlmap command is used to launch Sqlmap and specify the target URL, parameters, and other options required for the SQL injection attack. These are just a few examples of popular penetration testing tools and their uses, each providing unique capabilities and functionalities to support various aspects of penetration testing and security assessments. By leveraging these tools and incorporating them into their workflows, cybersecurity professionals can effectively identify and mitigate security vulnerabilities, protect sensitive data, and enhance the overall security posture of their organizations.

Chapter 6: Vulnerability Assessment and Management

Identifying vulnerabilities in networks and systems is a critical aspect of cybersecurity, enabling organizations to proactively assess and mitigate potential security risks that could be exploited by attackers. Vulnerabilities can exist in various components of a network or system, including software applications, operating systems, network devices, and configurations, making it essential for organizations to employ a comprehensive approach to vulnerability identification and management. One of the primary methods for identifying vulnerabilities in networks and systems is through vulnerability scanning, which involves the use of automated tools to scan target systems and networks for known vulnerabilities and misconfigurations. Vulnerability scanning tools such as Nessus, OpenVAS, and Qualys are commonly used to perform comprehensive scans of target systems and networks, identifying vulnerabilities in software applications, operating systems, and network devices. The nessus command is used to launch Nessus and initiate scans, while various options and settings can be configured to customize the scan parameters and reporting format. Similarly, the openvas command is used to launch OpenVAS and access its various scanning and reporting features. Another method for identifying vulnerabilities in networks and systems is through penetration testing, which involves simulating real-world attacks to identify security weaknesses and assess the effectiveness of existing security controls. Penetration testing tools such as Nmap, Metasploit, and Burp Suite are commonly used to conduct penetration tests, identifying vulnerabilities and exploiting them to gain unauthorized access to target systems and networks. The nmap command is used to launch Nmap and initiate scans, while various options and flags can be used to customize the scan parameters and output format. Additionally, the msfconsole command is used to launch the Metasploit framework, allowing users to interact with various modules and execute exploits against target systems. Vulnerability identification can also be performed manually through the use of specialized techniques and methodologies, such as code review, reverse engineering, and security assessments. Code review involves analyzing the source code of software applications to identify potential security vulnerabilities, such as buffer overflows, injection flaws, and insecure authentication mechanisms. Reverse engineering involves analyzing binary executables and firmware to understand how they work and identify potential vulnerabilities or backdoors. Security assessments involve reviewing the configuration settings and security controls of systems and networks to identify weaknesses and misconfigurations that could be exploited by attackers. In addition to automated scanning and manual techniques, organizations can also leverage threat intelligence feeds, security advisories, and vulnerability databases to stay informed about the latest security threats and vulnerabilities. These resources provide valuable information about known vulnerabilities, exploits, and attack techniques, allowing organizations to prioritize and address the most critical security issues first. By combining automated scanning, manual techniques, and threat intelligence, organizations can effectively identify vulnerabilities in networks and systems, enabling them to take proactive measures to mitigate potential security risks and protect sensitive data and resources from exploitation by attackers. Furthermore, vulnerability identification is an ongoing process that requires regular monitoring and updates to ensure that systems and networks remain secure against emerging threats and vulnerabilities. By continuously scanning for vulnerabilities, analyzing security logs, and applying patches and updates, organizations can reduce their exposure to cyber attacks and maintain a strong security posture in the face of evolving threats.

Vulnerability scanning techniques and tools are essential components of cybersecurity, enabling organizations to identify and mitigate potential security risks in their networks and systems. Vulnerability scanning involves the use of automated tools to scan target systems and networks for known vulnerabilities, misconfigurations, and security weaknesses that could be exploited by attackers. There are various vulnerability scanning techniques and tools available, each with its own strengths, capabilities, and methodologies. One of the most widely used vulnerability scanning tools is Nessus, a comprehensive vulnerability scanner that allows users to perform in-depth scans of target systems and networks to identify potential security vulnerabilities and compliance violations. The nessus command is used to launch Nessus and initiate scans, while various options and settings can be configured to customize the scan parameters and reporting format. Another popular vulnerability scanning tool is OpenVAS, an open-source vulnerability scanner that provides similar capabilities to Nessus, allowing users to perform comprehensive scans of target systems and networks to identify potential security vulnerabilities and misconfigurations. The openvas command is used to launch OpenVAS and access its various scanning and reporting features. Qualys is a cloud-based vulnerability management platform that provides vulnerability scanning, asset management, and compliance monitoring capabilities, allowing organizations to identify, prioritize, and remediate security vulnerabilities across their infrastructure. The qualys command is used to access the Qualys platform and initiate vulnerability scans, while various options and settings can be configured to customize the scan parameters and reporting format. Another vulnerability scanning tool is Nexpose, a vulnerability management solution that provides vulnerability assessment, risk prioritization, and remediation capabilities, allowing organizations to proactively manage and mitigate security risks across their infrastructure. The nexpose command is used to launch Nexpose and access its various scanning and reporting features. In addition to these commercial vulnerability scanning tools, there are also open-source vulnerability scanning tools available, such as OpenVAS, Nikto, and Lynis, which provide similar capabilities to their commercial counterparts but with the added benefit of being free and open-source. Nikto is a web server vulnerability scanner that allows users to scan web servers for common security issues such as outdated software, misconfigurations, and known vulnerabilities. The nikto command is used to launch Nikto and specify the target web server, port, and other scan parameters. Lynis is a security auditing tool that allows users to perform system hardening, compliance testing, and vulnerability scanning on Unix-based systems, providing recommendations and remediation steps for identified security issues. The lynis command is used to launch Lynis and initiate system audits and vulnerability scans. In addition to standalone vulnerability scanning tools, there are also vulnerability scanning services available, such as Tenable.io, Rapid7 InsightVM, and Qualys Cloud Platform, which provide cloud-based vulnerability scanning and management capabilities, allowing organizations to scan their infrastructure for security vulnerabilities and compliance violations without the need for dedicated on-premises infrastructure. These services offer scalable, on-demand vulnerability scanning capabilities, allowing organizations to quickly and easily identify and remediate security vulnerabilities across their infrastructure. Overall, vulnerability scanning techniques and tools are essential for organizations to proactively identify and mitigate potential security risks in their networks and systems, helping to protect sensitive data and resources from exploitation by attackers. By leveraging automated vulnerability scanning tools and services, organizations can ensure that their infrastructure remains secure and resilient against emerging threats and vulnerabilities.

Chapter 7: Web Application Security Testing

The OWASP Top 10 vulnerabilities are a list of the most critical security risks facing web applications, compiled by the Open Web Application Security Project (OWASP), a nonprofit organization dedicated to improving software security. The OWASP Top 10 provides guidance to organizations and developers on the most common and impactful security vulnerabilities in web applications, helping them prioritize and address security risks effectively. The OWASP Top 10 vulnerabilities are updated periodically to reflect emerging threats and changes in the security landscape, ensuring that the list remains relevant and actionable for organizations and developers. One of the most critical vulnerabilities in the OWASP Top 10 is Injection, which refers to security flaws that allow attackers to inject malicious code or commands into an application, leading to unauthorized access, data leakage, or denial of service. Common types of injection vulnerabilities include SQL injection, command injection, and LDAP injection, which can be exploited by attackers to manipulate databases, execute arbitrary commands, or compromise authentication mechanisms. The sqlmap command is used to launch Sqlmap and specify the target URL, parameters, and other options required for the SQL injection attack. Another critical vulnerability in the OWASP Top 10 is Broken Authentication, which refers to security flaws that allow attackers to bypass authentication mechanisms or hijack user sessions, leading to unauthorized access to sensitive data or functionality. Common examples of broken authentication vulnerabilities include weak passwords, insecure session management, and insufficient authentication controls, which can be exploited by attackers to compromise user accounts or impersonate legitimate users. The Burp Suite tool can be used to perform manual testing and identify broken authentication vulnerabilities by intercepting and modifying HTTP requests and responses, testing for session fixation, and analyzing authentication mechanisms. Cross-Site Scripting (XSS) is another critical vulnerability in the OWASP Top 10, which refers to security flaws that allow attackers to inject malicious scripts into web pages viewed by other users, leading to the theft of sensitive information or the execution of arbitrary code in the context of the victim's browser. The OWASP ZAP tool is a popular open-source security scanner that can be used to detect and exploit XSS vulnerabilities by sending malicious payloads to web applications and analyzing the responses for evidence of successful exploitation. Insecure Direct Object References (IDOR) is another critical vulnerability in the OWASP Top 10, which refers to security flaws that allow attackers to manipulate references to sensitive objects in web applications, leading to unauthorized access to sensitive data or functionality. The idor command is used to launch IDOR attacks and manipulate object references in web applications, such as changing the value of a parameter in a URL or form submission to access another user's data or perform unauthorized actions. Security Misconfiguration is another critical vulnerability in the OWASP Top 10, which refers to security flaws that arise from improper configuration settings or default configurations in web applications, leading to unauthorized access, data leakage, or denial of service. Common examples of security misconfigurations include open ports, default passwords, and unnecessary services or features enabled by default, which can be exploited by attackers to compromise web applications or underlying infrastructure. The Nmap tool is a powerful network scanning tool that can be used to identify open ports and services on target systems and networks, allowing organizations to detect security misconfigurations and take appropriate remediation actions to mitigate security risks. These are just a few examples of the critical vulnerabilities in the OWASP Top 10, each representing a significant security risk to web applications and organizations. By understanding and addressing these vulnerabilities effectively, organizations can improve the security posture of their web applications and reduce the risk of exploitation by attackers. Testing web application security involves a variety of techniques and methodologies aimed at identifying and mitigating vulnerabilities and security risks in web applications, ensuring that they remain resilient against cyber attacks and unauthorized access. One of the primary techniques for testing web application security is penetration testing, which involves simulating real-world attacks to identify security weaknesses and assess the effectiveness of existing security controls. Penetration testing tools such as Burp Suite, OWASP ZAP, and Metasploit are commonly used to conduct penetration tests, allowing testers to identify vulnerabilities and exploit them to gain unauthorized access to target web applications. The burpsuite command is used to launch Burp Suite and access its various tools and features, including the Proxy, Scanner, Intruder, Repeater, and Sequencer, while the zap command is used to launch OWASP ZAP and initiate scans and attacks against target web applications. Metasploit is a powerful penetration testing framework that provides a wide range of exploits, payloads, and auxiliary modules for testing the security of web applications, allowing testers to simulate attacks such as SQL injection, cross-site scripting (XSS), and remote code execution. The msfconsole command is used to launch Metasploit and interact with various modules and execute exploits against target systems. Another technique for testing web application security is vulnerability scanning, which involves the use of automated tools to scan target web applications for known vulnerabilities, misconfigurations, and security weaknesses. Vulnerability scanning tools such as Nessus, OpenVAS, and Qualys are commonly used to perform comprehensive scans of target web applications, identifying vulnerabilities in software applications, operating systems, and network devices. The nessus command is used to launch Nessus and initiate scans, while various options and settings can be configured to customize the scan parameters and reporting format. Similarly, the openvas command is used to launch OpenVAS and access its various scanning and reporting features, while the qualys command is used to access the Qualys platform and initiate vulnerability scans. In addition to penetration testing and vulnerability scanning, another technique for testing web application security is code review, which involves analyzing the source code of web applications to identify potential security vulnerabilities and coding errors. Code review tools such as Fortify, Veracode, and Checkmarx are commonly used to perform static code analysis, allowing testers to identify security flaws such as injection vulnerabilities, authentication bypasses, and insecure cryptographic algorithms. These tools analyze the source code of web applications and provide detailed reports and remediation recommendations for identified security issues. The fortify command is used to launch Fortify and initiate static code analysis, while the veracode command is used to access the Veracode platform and submit code for analysis, and the checkmarx command is used to launch Checkmarx and perform static code analysis. Another technique for testing web application security is dynamic analysis, which involves analyzing the behavior of web applications in real-time to identify potential security vulnerabilities and weaknesses. Dynamic analysis tools such as AppScan, WebInspect, and

Acunetix are commonly used to perform dynamic analysis of web applications, allowing testers to identify vulnerabilities such as SQL injection, cross-site scripting (XSS), and directory traversal. These tools simulate attacks against target web applications and analyze their responses for evidence of successful exploitation. The appscan command is used to launch AppScan and initiate dynamic analysis, while the webinspect command is used to launch WebInspect and perform dynamic analysis of target web applications, and the acunetix command is used to access the Acunetix platform and initiate scans. Additionally, manual testing techniques such as fuzz testing, parameter tampering, and session hijacking can be used to identify security vulnerabilities and weaknesses in web applications. Fuzz testing involves sending malformed or unexpected input to target web applications to identify potential security vulnerabilities and coding errors. Parameter tampering involves manipulating input parameters in HTTP requests to bypass input validation and access unauthorized functionality. Session hijacking involves intercepting and manipulating session cookies or tokens to gain unauthorized access to target web applications. These manual testing techniques can be performed using tools such as Burp Suite, OWASP

ZAP, and Wireshark, allowing testers to identify security vulnerabilities and weaknesses in target web applications. Overall, testing web application security involves a variety of techniques and methodologies aimed at identifying and mitigating vulnerabilities and security risks in web applications, ensuring that they remain resilient against cyber attacks and unauthorized access. By leveraging penetration testing, vulnerability scanning, code review, dynamic analysis, and manual testing techniques, organizations can improve the security posture of their web applications and reduce the risk of exploitation by attackers.

Chapter 8: Wireless Network Security

Wireless encryption protocols play a crucial role in securing wireless networks, protecting sensitive data from unauthorized access and interception. One of the earliest wireless encryption protocols is Wired Equivalent Privacy (WEP), which was introduced in the late 1990s to provide security for wireless networks. WEP encrypts data transmitted over the wireless network using the RC4 encryption algorithm, with a fixed-length 40-bit or 104-bit encryption key. However, WEP has several significant security vulnerabilities that make it susceptible to attacks, including the weakness of the RC4 encryption algorithm, the predictability of initialization vectors (IVs), and the lack of key management mechanisms. As a result, WEP is no longer considered secure and is not recommended for use in wireless networks. Instead, organizations should use more secure encryption protocols such as Wi-Fi Protected Access (WPA) and Wi-Fi Protected Access 2 (WPA2). WPA was introduced as an interim security enhancement to WEP, addressing some of its security weaknesses while maintaining compatibility with existing hardware. WPA uses the Temporal Key Integrity Protocol (TKIP) encryption algorithm, which provides stronger encryption than WEP and addresses vulnerabilities such as IV reuse and key management. Additionally, WPA introduces the use of the Message Integrity Check (MIC) to detect and prevent tampering with data packets. To deploy WPA encryption on a wireless network, users can configure their wireless access points and client devices to use WPA encryption and specify a pre-shared key (PSK) or use an authentication server such as RADIUS for enterprise deployments. The wpa_supplicant command is used to configure WPA encryption on Linux-based systems, allowing users to specify the SSID of the wireless network, the encryption protocol (WPA or WPA2), and the authentication method (PSK or EAP). WPA2 is the current standard for wireless encryption and provides stronger security than WPA by using the Advanced Encryption Standard (AES) encryption algorithm, which is considered more secure than TKIP. WPA2 also introduces additional security features such as stronger key management mechanisms and support for stronger authentication methods such as Extensible Authentication Protocol (EAP). To deploy WPA2 encryption on a wireless network, users can configure their wireless access points and client devices to use WPA2 encryption and specify a pre-shared key (PSK) or use an authentication server such as RADIUS for enterprise deployments. The wpa_supplicant command can also be used to configure WPA2 encryption on Linux-based systems, allowing users to specify the SSID of the wireless network, the encryption protocol (WPA2), and the authentication method (PSK or EAP). In addition to WPA and WPA2, the Wi-Fi Alliance has introduced a new wireless encryption protocol called Wi-Fi Protected Access 3 (WPA3), which provides even stronger security features and protections against emerging threats. WPA3 introduces several security enhancements, including stronger encryption for personal and enterprise networks, protection against brute-force attacks on the pre-shared key (PSK), and simplified configuration for IoT devices with limited user interfaces. WPA3 also introduces new security features such as Opportunistic Wireless Encryption (OWE), which provides encryption for open Wi-Fi networks without the need for a pre-shared key (PSK) or authentication server. To deploy WPA3 encryption on a wireless network, users can configure their wireless access points and client devices to use WPA3 encryption and specify the appropriate security features and settings. The wpa_supplicant command may be updated to support WPA3 encryption on Linux-based systems, allowing users to specify the SSID of the wireless network, the encryption protocol (WPA3), and any additional security features or settings. Overall, wireless encryption protocols such as WEP, WPA, WPA2, and WPA3 play a critical role in securing wireless networks and protecting sensitive data from unauthorized access and interception. By deploying strong encryption protocols and implementing appropriate security measures, organizations can ensure that their wireless networks remain secure against cyber attacks and data breaches. Wireless attack vectors pose significant security risks to organizations, as wireless networks are inherently more vulnerable to attacks than wired networks due to their broadcast nature and lack of physical boundaries. Attackers can exploit vulnerabilities in wireless networks to gain unauthorized access, intercept sensitive data, and launch various types of cyber attacks. One common wireless attack vector is eavesdropping, where attackers intercept and monitor wireless communications to capture sensitive information such as passwords, usernames, and financial data. Eavesdropping attacks can be mitigated by encrypting wireless communications using strong encryption protocols such as WPA2 or WPA3. Another wireless attack vector is rogue access points, where attackers set up unauthorized wireless access points to trick users into connecting to them, allowing attackers to intercept and manipulate network traffic. To mitigate rogue access point attacks, organizations should implement wireless intrusion detection systems (WIDS) or wireless intrusion prevention systems (WIPS) to detect and block unauthorized access points. The airodump-ng command is a powerful tool for scanning wireless networks and identifying rogue access points, allowing organizations to monitor their wireless environments for unauthorized devices. Denial-of-Service (DoS) attacks are another common wireless attack vector, where attackers flood wireless networks with traffic or deauthenticate legitimate users, causing network outages and disrupting communication. To mitigate DoS attacks, organizations can implement rate limiting and access control mechanisms on their wireless access points to limit the amount of traffic allowed on the network. Additionally, organizations can deploy intrusion detection and prevention systems (IDS/IPS) to detect and block malicious traffic associated with DoS attacks. The aireplay-ng command is used to launch deauthentication attacks against wireless clients, allowing attackers to disconnect legitimate users from the network and disrupt communication. Man-in-the-Middle (MitM) attacks are another significant wireless attack vector, where attackers intercept and manipulate wireless communications between two parties, allowing them to eavesdrop on sensitive information or impersonate legitimate users. To mitigate MitM attacks, organizations should use strong encryption protocols such as WPA2 or WPA3 to encrypt wireless communications and protect against interception and tampering. Additionally, organizations can implement certificate-based authentication mechanisms to verify the identity of wireless clients and servers, preventing attackers from impersonating legitimate entities. The sslstrip command is a tool used to launch MitM attacks against HTTPS connections, allowing attackers to intercept and modify encrypted web traffic. Evil Twin attacks are a variant of rogue access point attacks, where attackers set up fake wireless access points with the same SSID as legitimate networks to trick users into connecting to them. Once connected, attackers can intercept and manipulate network traffic or launch other types of attacks. To mitigate Evil Twin attacks, organizations should educate users about the risks of connecting to unknown wireless networks and implement strong authentication mechanisms such as certificate-based authentication to verify the identity of wireless access points. Additionally, organizations can use wireless intrusion detection and prevention systems (WIDS/WIPS) to detect and block Evil Twin access points. The airbase-ng command is used to create fake wireless access points for Evil Twin attacks, allowing attackers to trick users into connecting to them. Wi-Fi Protected Setup (WPS) attacks are another significant wireless attack vector, where attackers exploit vulnerabilities in the WPS protocol to gain unauthorized access to wireless networks. To mitigate WPS attacks, organizations should disable WPS on their wireless access points or use strong, randomly generated PINs to prevent brute-force attacks. Additionally, organizations can use wireless intrusion detection and prevention systems (WIDS/WIPS) to detect and block WPS attacks. The reaver command is a tool used to launch brute-force attacks against WPS-enabled wireless access points, allowing attackers to recover the WPS PIN and gain unauthorized access to the network. Overall, wireless attack vectors pose significant security risks to organizations, but by implementing appropriate countermeasures and security best practices, organizations can mitigate these risks and protect their wireless networks from cyber attacks.

Chapter 9: Social Engineering Techniques

Social engineering relies on psychological principles to manipulate individuals into divulging confidential information, granting unauthorized access, or performing actions that compromise security. One such principle is authority, where individuals are more likely to comply with requests from perceived authority figures. Attackers exploit this principle by impersonating trusted entities such as IT administrators, law enforcement officers, or company executives to gain compliance from unsuspecting victims. Another psychological principle leveraged in social engineering is urgency, where individuals are more inclined to act quickly in response to urgent requests or emergencies. Attackers create a sense of urgency by fabricating scenarios such as security breaches, account compromises, or impending deadlines to pressure victims into disclosing sensitive information or bypassing security controls. Additionally, social proof is a psychological principle that influences individuals to follow the actions of others, especially in uncertain situations. Attackers exploit social proof by fabricating social cues such as fake testimonials, user reviews, or endorsements to convince victims to trust their requests or recommendations. Reciprocity is another psychological principle used in social engineering, where individuals feel obligated to reciprocate favors or concessions received from others. Attackers exploit reciprocity by offering small gifts, compliments, or assistance to victims to establish rapport and increase the likelihood of compliance with subsequent requests. Moreover, scarcity is a psychological principle that drives individuals to place greater value on items or opportunities that are perceived as scarce or limited. Attackers create a sense of scarcity by fabricating scenarios such as limited-time offers, exclusive access, or high demand to motivate victims to take immediate action without questioning the legitimacy of requests. Furthermore, familiarity is a psychological principle that influences individuals to trust and feel comfortable with familiar stimuli or situations. Attackers exploit familiarity by using social engineering techniques such as pretexting or phishing emails that mimic familiar communication styles, language, or branding to deceive victims into disclosing sensitive information or performing unauthorized actions. Social engineering attacks often begin with reconnaissance, where attackers gather information about potential targets to tailor their approaches and increase the likelihood of success. Social media platforms, company websites, and public databases are common sources of information used by attackers to gather personal details, job roles, relationships, and interests of potential victims. The information obtained during reconnaissance is then used to craft convincing pretexting scenarios or phishing messages that exploit psychological vulnerabilities and elicit desired responses from victims. Pretexting is a social engineering technique where attackers create a fabricated pretext or scenario to manipulate individuals into divulging confidential information or performing specific actions. Attackers may pose as trusted entities such as IT support personnel, vendors, or coworkers to gain the trust and cooperation of unsuspecting victims. Phishing is another prevalent social engineering technique where attackers use deceptive emails, text messages, or phone calls to trick individuals into disclosing sensitive information such as login credentials, financial data, or personal details. Phishing emails often employ psychological tactics such as urgency, fear, curiosity, or authority to persuade recipients to click on malicious links, download malicious attachments, or provide sensitive information. Spear phishing is a targeted form of phishing where attackers tailor their messages to specific individuals or organizations based on information obtained during reconnaissance. Spear phishing emails often appear more personalized and credible, increasing the likelihood of success compared to generic phishing campaigns. Vishing, or voice phishing, is a social engineering technique where attackers use phone calls to deceive individuals into revealing sensitive information or performing specific actions. Attackers may impersonate trusted entities such as bank representatives, government officials, or technical support personnel to gain the trust and cooperation of victims. Smishing, or SMS phishing, is a social engineering technique where attackers use text messages to deceive individuals into disclosing sensitive information or clicking on malicious links. Smishing messages often impersonate legitimate organizations or services and contain urgent requests or enticing offers to lure victims into taking action. Ultimately, social engineering exploits psychological vulnerabilities to manipulate individuals into divulging confidential information, granting unauthorized access, or performing actions that compromise security. By understanding the psychological principles behind social engineering and implementing security awareness training, organizations can empower employees to recognize and resist social engineering attacks, thereby reducing the risk of successful exploitation.

Social engineering, a cornerstone of cyber attacks, hinges on exploiting human psychology to gain unauthorized access to systems, data, or information. One of the fundamental psychological principles underpinning social engineering is trust. Trust plays a pivotal role in human interactions, and attackers exploit this innate tendency to trust others to manipulate victims into divulging sensitive information or performing actions that compromise security. Attackers often leverage various tactics to establish trust, such as impersonating trusted individuals or organizations, forging credentials, or creating convincing pretexts. Authority is another potent psychological principle that social engineers exploit to manipulate victims. Individuals are predisposed to comply with requests from perceived authority figures, making them susceptible to manipulation by attackers posing as supervisors, IT administrators, or law enforcement officials. Attackers capitalize on this tendency by leveraging authority to elicit compliance with their demands, whether it be disclosing sensitive information, granting access privileges, or executing malicious commands. Similarly, urgency is a psychological principle that social engineers exploit to elicit rapid responses from their targets. Urgent situations trigger instinctive responses in individuals, often bypassing rational thought processes and leading to impulsive actions. Attackers fabricate scenarios that instill a sense of urgency in their victims, such as impending deadlines, security breaches, or financial emergencies, compelling them to act hastily without critically evaluating the legitimacy of requests. Social proof, the tendency to follow the actions of others in ambiguous situations, is another psychological principle exploited by social engineers. By creating the illusion of social consensus or legitimacy, attackers persuade individuals to comply with their requests, even if they harbor doubts or suspicions. Attackers may fabricate social cues, such as fake testimonials, user reviews, or endorsements, to bolster the credibility of their requests and manipulate victims into trusting them. Reciprocity, the inclination to reciprocate favors or concessions received from others, is a psychological principle that social engineers leverage to establish rapport with their targets. By offering small gifts, compliments, or assistance, attackers create a sense of indebtedness in their victims, fostering a willingness to reciprocate by complying with subsequent requests or demands. Scarcity, the perception that resources or opportunities are limited, is another psychological principle exploited by social engineers to manipulate individuals. By creating artificial scarcity or urgency around their offers or requests, attackers compel individuals to act quickly to secure perceived benefits or avoid missing out on opportunities. Familiarity, the preference for familiar stimuli or situations, is a psychological principle that social engineers exploit to lower victims' defenses and elicit compliance. Attackers mimic familiar communication styles, language, or branding to create a sense of familiarity and trust, thereby increasing the likelihood of successful manipulation. To deploy social engineering tactics effectively, attackers often conduct extensive reconnaissance to gather information about their targets. This reconnaissance phase may involve scouring social media profiles, company websites, public databases, or online forums to gather personal details, job roles, relationships, and interests of potential victims. Armed with this information, attackers tailor their social engineering tactics to exploit specific psychological vulnerabilities and increase the likelihood of success. Pretexting, a common social engineering technique, involves creating a fabricated pretext or scenario to deceive victims into divulging sensitive information or performing specific actions. Attackers may pose as trusted entities, such as IT support personnel, vendors, or coworkers, to gain the trust and cooperation of unsuspecting victims. Phishing, perhaps the most prevalent social engineering technique, relies on deceptive emails, text messages, or phone calls to trick individuals into disclosing sensitive information or downloading malware. Attackers craft convincing messages that exploit psychological triggers such as urgency, fear, curiosity, or authority to persuade recipients to click on malicious links, provide login credentials, or transfer funds. Spear phishing, a targeted variant of phishing, involves tailoring messages to specific individuals or organizations based on information obtained during reconnaissance. These personalized messages appear more credible and increase the likelihood of successful exploitation. Vishing, or voice phishing, is a social engineering technique that uses phone calls to deceive individuals into revealing sensitive information or performing specific actions. Attackers may impersonate trusted entities, such as bank representatives or technical support personnel, to gain the trust and cooperation of victims. Smishing, or SMS phishing, leverages text messages to deceive individuals into disclosing sensitive information or clicking on malicious links. Attackers craft enticing messages that exploit psychological triggers to lure victims into taking actions that compromise security. In summary, social engineering is a potent tactic in the arsenal of cyber attackers, relying on the manipulation of human psychology to exploit vulnerabilities and circumvent traditional security measures. By understanding the psychological principles behind social engineering and implementing robust security awareness training programs, organizations can empower employees to recognize and resist manipulation attempts, thereby reducing the risk of successful exploitation.

Chapter 10: Penetration Testing Reporting and Documentation

A penetration testing report is a critical deliverable that provides detailed findings, analysis, and recommendations resulting from a penetration test. The report serves as a comprehensive record of the test methodology, vulnerabilities discovered, exploitation techniques used, and remediation guidance offered. One of the essential components of a penetration testing report is the Executive Summary, which provides a high-level overview of the test objectives, scope, findings, and recommendations in a concise format suitable for executive stakeholders. The Executive Summary summarizes key findings, identifies critical vulnerabilities, and highlights remediation priorities to help decision-makers understand the security posture of the organization and prioritize remediation efforts accordingly. Another crucial component of a penetration testing report is the Methodology section, which outlines the approach, tools, and techniques used during the test. The Methodology section provides insight into the testing process, including reconnaissance, vulnerability identification, exploitation, and post-exploitation activities. It describes the tools and scripts used to automate tasks, capture evidence, and validate findings, such as Nmap for network scanning, Burp Suite for web application testing, or Metasploit for exploit development and execution. Furthermore, the Findings section of a penetration testing report details the vulnerabilities discovered during the test, including their severity, impact, and exploitability. Vulnerabilities are typically categorized based on their risk level, such as critical, high, medium, or low, and accompanied by detailed descriptions, proof-of-concept exploit code, and remediation recommendations. The Findings section may include screenshots, network diagrams, or log excerpts to provide context and evidence of the identified vulnerabilities. Additionally, the Recommendations section of a penetration testing report offers actionable guidance on how to remediate the identified vulnerabilities and improve overall security posture. Recommendations are prioritized based on risk level, feasibility, and impact on the organization, with clear instructions for implementing security controls, patches, or configuration changes to mitigate identified risks. Recommendations may also include suggestions for improving security policies, procedures, or employee training to prevent future security incidents. Moreover, the Appendices section of a penetration testing report contains supplementary information, such as detailed technical notes, raw scan results, log files, or additional documentation relevant to the test. Appendices provide readers with additional context and resources to better understand the test methodology, findings, and remediation recommendations. They may include references to industry standards, best practices, or regulatory requirements to support the validity and credibility of the report findings. Furthermore, the Conclusion section of a penetration testing report summarizes key takeaways, lessons learned, and next steps following the test. The Conclusion section highlights the overall effectiveness of security controls, areas for improvement, and recommendations for future testing or risk management initiatives. It provides a final assessment of the organization's security posture and outlines the path forward for addressing identified vulnerabilities and strengthening security defenses. Additionally, the Glossary section of a penetration testing report defines technical terms, acronyms, or jargon used throughout the report to ensure clarity and understanding for readers. The Glossary helps stakeholders, including non-technical audiences, interpret the report findings and recommendations accurately and facilitates communication between security professionals and business stakeholders. Furthermore, the References section of a penetration testing report cites sources, references, or external documentation used to support the findings, analysis, and recommendations presented in the report. References may include security advisories, vendor documentation, research papers, or regulatory guidelines relevant to the identified vulnerabilities and remediation strategies. They provide readers with additional context and resources for further investigation or validation of the report findings. In summary, a penetration testing report comprises several key components, including the Executive Summary, Methodology, Findings, Recommendations, Appendices, Conclusion, Glossary, and References, each serving a distinct purpose in communicating the results of the test and guiding remediation efforts to improve security posture.

Clear and effective documentation is essential for ensuring that information is accurately communicated, understood, and utilized by stakeholders. One of the best practices for clear and effective documentation is to maintain consistency in formatting, structure, and terminology throughout the document. Consistent documentation helps readers navigate the content more easily, understand complex concepts, and locate specific information quickly. Another best practice is to use descriptive and concise language to convey information clearly and accurately. Avoiding jargon, technical terms, or ambiguous language helps ensure that readers can understand the documentation regardless of their level of expertise or familiarity with the subject matter. Additionally, organizing the documentation into logical sections, headings, and subheadings can help readers navigate the document more efficiently and find the information they need. Using bullet points, numbered lists, or tables to present information in a structured format can also improve readability and comprehension. Moreover, providing examples, illustrations, or screenshots can help clarify concepts, demonstrate procedures, and reinforce key points. Visual aids can enhance understanding, especially for complex topics or processes, by providing visual representations of information that complement the text. Another best practice for clear and effective documentation is to incorporate feedback from stakeholders to ensure that the documentation meets their needs and addresses their concerns. Soliciting feedback from end users, subject matter experts, or other stakeholders can help identify areas for improvement, clarify ambiguities, and correct errors or inaccuracies in the documentation. Additionally, documenting revision history, versioning, or change logs can help stakeholders track updates, changes, and revisions to the documentation over time. Version control systems, such as Git or Subversion, can facilitate collaborative editing, revision tracking, and versioning of documentation, ensuring that stakeholders have access to the most up-to-date information. Furthermore, ensuring that documentation is easily accessible and searchable can enhance usability and facilitate knowledge sharing among stakeholders. Providing multiple formats, such as PDF, HTML, or Markdown, can accommodate different preferences and accessibility needs. Additionally, using metadata, tags, or keywords can improve searchability and help users locate relevant documentation quickly using search engines or document management systems. Moreover, documenting assumptions, dependencies, or constraints can help set expectations, clarify requirements, and mitigate risks associated with the information or processes described in the documentation. Clearly stating assumptions or constraints helps readers understand the context and limitations of the information presented and prevents misunderstandings or misinterpretations. Additionally, documenting the rationale or reasoning behind decisions, recommendations, or design choices can help stakeholders understand the thought process and considerations that informed the documentation. Providing context or background information can help readers understand the significance, relevance, and implications of the information presented in the documentation. Moreover, documenting best practices, guidelines, or standards can help ensure consistency, quality, and compliance with organizational policies or industry regulations. Clearly articulating best practices or standards helps stakeholders understand expectations, align with established norms, and adhere to established guidelines when performing tasks or making decisions. Furthermore, incorporating documentation into the development process, such as creating documentation templates, checklists, or guidelines, can help streamline documentation efforts and ensure that documentation is consistently created and updated throughout the project lifecycle. Integrating documentation into development workflows, such as code repositories, issue trackers, or project management tools, can help ensure that documentation remains up-to-date and relevant as the project evolves. Additionally, providing training or resources to stakeholders on how to create, maintain, and use documentation effectively can help promote a culture of documentation and knowledge sharing within the organization. Offering workshops, tutorials, or documentation guides can help stakeholders develop the skills and knowledge needed to produce high-quality documentation and leverage documentation resources effectively. In summary, clear and effective documentation is essential for communicating information accurately, facilitating understanding, and enabling stakeholders to make informed decisions. By following best practices such as maintaining consistency, using descriptive language, organizing content logically, incorporating feedback, ensuring accessibility, documenting assumptions, providing context, articulating best practices, integrating documentation into development workflows, and providing training and resources, organizations can create documentation that is clear, concise, and actionable.

BOOK 2
PENTEST+ EXAM PASS
ADVANCED TECHNIQUES AND TOOLS

ROB BOTWRIGHT

Chapter 1: Advanced Reconnaissance Strategies

Leveraging open-source intelligence (OSINT) for targeted reconnaissance is a crucial aspect of cybersecurity operations, enabling organizations to gather valuable information about potential threats, vulnerabilities, and adversaries from publicly available sources. One of the primary techniques used in OSINT reconnaissance is passive information gathering, which involves collecting data from publicly accessible sources without directly interacting with the target. Passive information gathering techniques include conducting domain name searches using tools like WHOIS or DNSDumpster to gather information about domain ownership, registration dates, and associated IP addresses. Additionally, passive reconnaissance may involve searching for information on social media platforms, forums, or online communities to gather insights into an organization's personnel, activities, technologies, or relationships. Furthermore, OSINT reconnaissance often involves analyzing metadata associated with digital assets such as documents, images, or videos to extract valuable information such as author names, creation dates, or geolocation data. Tools like ExifTool or Metadata Analyzer can be used to extract and analyze metadata from digital files, providing insights into the origin, history, or context of the assets. Moreover, OSINT reconnaissance may involve analyzing publicly available network data, such as routing tables, BGP announcements, or SSL certificate transparency logs, to identify potential attack vectors, misconfigurations, or vulnerabilities in an organization's infrastructure. Tools like Shodan or Censys can be used to search for exposed network devices, services, or protocols, providing valuable insights into an organization's attack surface and potential security risks. Additionally, OSINT reconnaissance often involves analyzing publicly available code repositories, such as GitHub or GitLab, to identify leaked credentials, sensitive information, or vulnerable code that could be exploited by attackers. Tools like Gitrob or truffleHog can be used to search code repositories for secrets, API keys, or other sensitive information that may have been inadvertently exposed. Furthermore, OSINT reconnaissance may involve analyzing publicly available threat intelligence feeds, such as the Mitre ATT&CK framework or the Open Source Vulnerability Database (OSVDB), to identify known threats, vulnerabilities, or adversary tactics that may pose a risk to an organization. By monitoring threat intelligence feeds, organizations can stay informed about emerging threats, vulnerabilities, or attack trends and take proactive measures to mitigate risks and enhance their security posture. Moreover, OSINT reconnaissance may involve analyzing publicly available threat actor profiles, such as those on forums, social media platforms, or dark web marketplaces, to gather intelligence about potential adversaries, their capabilities, motivations, and tactics. By monitoring threat actor profiles, organizations can identify emerging threats, track adversary activity, and anticipate potential attacks, allowing them to take preemptive action to defend against cyber threats. Additionally, OSINT reconnaissance may involve analyzing publicly available news articles, reports, or blog posts to gather information about security incidents, data breaches, or regulatory compliance issues that may affect an organization's security posture. By monitoring news sources and industry reports, organizations can stay informed about emerging threats, trends, and best practices in cybersecurity, allowing them to adapt their security strategies and mitigate risks accordingly. Furthermore, OSINT reconnaissance may involve conducting online searches using advanced search operators and techniques to gather targeted information about specific topics, keywords, or entities. Advanced search operators, such as site:, intitle:, or filetype:, can be used to narrow down search results and focus on specific types of information or sources. Additionally, OSINT reconnaissance may involve leveraging data analysis and visualization tools to process, analyze, and visualize large volumes of data collected during reconnaissance activities. Tools like Maltego or SpiderFoot can be used to aggregate data from multiple sources, correlate information, and identify relationships or patterns that may be relevant to the investigation. Moreover, OSINT reconnaissance may involve conducting social engineering attacks, such as phishing or pretexting, to gather information from individuals or organizations. Social engineering attacks leverage psychological manipulation techniques to deceive individuals into revealing sensitive information, such as passwords, credentials, or proprietary data. By exploiting human vulnerabilities, social engineering attacks can bypass technical controls and gain access to valuable information or resources. Additionally, OSINT reconnaissance may involve analyzing publicly available satellite imagery or geospatial data to gather intelligence about physical locations, infrastructure, or assets. Satellite imagery can provide valuable insights into the layout, topology, or vulnerabilities of an organization's facilities, allowing security teams to assess risks and plan mitigation strategies accordingly. In summary, leveraging OSINT for targeted reconnaissance is a critical component of cybersecurity operations, enabling organizations to gather valuable intelligence about potential threats, vulnerabilities, and adversaries from publicly available sources. By employing a combination of passive information gathering techniques, data analysis tools, threat intelligence feeds, and social engineering tactics, organizations can enhance their situational awareness, identify emerging threats, and take proactive measures to protect their assets and data from cyber attacks. Advanced network mapping techniques play a crucial role in cybersecurity operations, enabling organizations to gain comprehensive visibility into their network infrastructure, identify potential vulnerabilities, and enhance their overall security posture. One of the advanced network mapping techniques widely used is active reconnaissance, which involves actively probing network devices and services to discover and enumerate hosts, ports, and protocols. Tools like Nmap or Masscan can be used to perform active reconnaissance by sending probe packets to target hosts and analyzing the responses to identify live hosts, open ports, and running services. Additionally, active reconnaissance may involve performing service fingerprinting to identify specific software versions, configurations, or vulnerabilities associated with detected services. Tools like Bannergrab or Netcat can be used to connect to open ports and retrieve banners or service information that can be used to fingerprint services and identify potential vulnerabilities. Another advanced network mapping technique is passive reconnaissance, which involves monitoring network traffic passively to gather information about network devices, communications, and behaviors without directly interacting with the target network. Passive reconnaissance techniques include network sniffing, packet capture, and traffic analysis, which can be performed using tools like Wireshark or tcpdump. By analyzing network traffic, organizations can gain insights into network topology, traffic patterns, and communication protocols, helping them identify potential security risks and anomalies. Furthermore, advanced network mapping techniques may involve performing topology discovery to map out the physical and logical structure of a network, including routers, switches, subnets, VLANs, and interconnections. Tools like SNMPWalk or CDP (Cisco Discovery Protocol) can be used to query network devices for information about their neighbors, interfaces, and routing tables, helping organizations visualize the network topology and identify potential points of failure or misconfiguration. Additionally, advanced network mapping techniques may involve performing protocol analysis to identify protocol-specific vulnerabilities, misconfigurations, or anomalies that may be exploited by attackers. Tools like Wireshark or Zeek (formerly known as Bro) can be used to capture and analyze network traffic at the protocol level, allowing organizations to identify suspicious behaviors, protocol violations, or security weaknesses that may indicate an ongoing attack or compromise. Moreover, advanced network mapping techniques may involve performing vulnerability scanning to identify known vulnerabilities, misconfigurations, or weaknesses in network devices, applications, or services. Tools like Nessus, OpenVAS, or Qualys can be used to scan network hosts for known vulnerabilities, assess their severity, and prioritize remediation efforts based on risk level. Vulnerability scanning helps organizations proactively identify and address security weaknesses before they can be exploited by attackers. Furthermore, advanced network mapping techniques may involve performing network reconnaissance using social engineering tactics to gather information about network devices, users, or security controls through human interaction. Social engineering techniques include phishing, pretexting, or impersonation, which can be used to trick employees into revealing sensitive information, credentials, or access privileges that can be leveraged to compromise the network. By combining social engineering tactics with technical reconnaissance techniques, attackers can gather comprehensive intelligence about an organization's network infrastructure, assets, and security posture, increasing the likelihood of a successful attack. Additionally, advanced network mapping techniques may involve leveraging threat intelligence feeds, open-source intelligence (OSINT), or dark web monitoring to gather information about emerging threats, attack trends, or adversary tactics that may pose a risk to the network. By monitoring external sources of intelligence, organizations can stay informed about potential threats and take proactive measures to defend against cyber attacks. Moreover, advanced network mapping techniques may involve performing active reconnaissance using specialized tools and techniques to evade detection, bypass security controls, or gather intelligence covertly. Techniques such as port knocking, stealth scanning, or tunneling can be used to conceal reconnaissance activities and avoid triggering intrusion detection or prevention systems. By employing stealthy reconnaissance techniques, attackers can gather information about a target network without alerting defenders or raising suspicion, increasing their chances of success. In summary, advanced network mapping techniques play a vital role in cybersecurity operations, enabling organizations to gain visibility into their network infrastructure, identify potential vulnerabilities, and mitigate security risks. By combining active and passive reconnaissance techniques, protocol analysis, vulnerability scanning, social engineering tactics, threat intelligence, and evasion techniques, organizations can develop a comprehensive understanding of their network environment and implement effective security measures to protect against cyber threats.

Chapter 2: Exploiting Network Protocols

A deep dive into common network protocols is essential for understanding how data is transmitted, received, and processed across computer networks, enabling organizations to design, deploy, and secure their network infrastructure effectively. One of the most widely used network protocols is the Internet Protocol (IP), which forms the foundation of the Internet and enables communication between devices connected to the network. The IP protocol defines how data packets are addressed, routed, and delivered to their destination, using unique IP addresses assigned to each device on the network. Within the IP protocol suite, there are two main versions in use today: IPv4 and IPv6. IPv4, the fourth version of the Internet Protocol, uses 32-bit addresses and is the most widely deployed version of IP, although its address space is becoming increasingly depleted due to the growth of the Internet. Conversely, IPv6, the sixth version of the Internet Protocol, uses 128-bit addresses and provides a vastly expanded address space, enabling the continued growth of the Internet and support for emerging technologies such as Internet of Things (IoT) devices. Another crucial network protocol is the Transmission Control Protocol (TCP), which operates at the transport layer of the OSI model and provides reliable, connection-oriented communication between devices over the network. TCP ensures that data is transmitted reliably by establishing a connection between sender and receiver, segmenting data into packets, numbering packets for sequencing, and implementing flow control and error detection mechanisms to ensure data integrity and delivery. TCP is widely used for applications that require guaranteed delivery of data, such as web browsing, email, file transfer, and remote access. Additionally, the User Datagram Protocol (UDP) is another important network protocol that operates at the transport layer and provides connectionless, unreliable communication between devices over the network. Unlike TCP, UDP does not establish a connection before transmitting data and does not guarantee delivery or order of packets. Instead, UDP is used for applications that prioritize speed and efficiency over reliability, such as real-time multimedia streaming, online gaming, and DNS (Domain Name System) resolution. Moving up the OSI model, the Hypertext Transfer Protocol (HTTP) is a fundamental application-layer protocol used for transmitting and receiving web-based content over the Internet. HTTP defines how web browsers and web servers communicate by exchanging requests and responses containing hypertext documents, such as HTML pages, images, scripts, and stylesheets. HTTP operates over TCP, typically using port 80 for unencrypted communication or port 443 for encrypted communication (HTTPS). Additionally, the Domain Name System (DNS) is a critical network protocol used for translating domain names into IP addresses and vice versa, enabling users to access websites and services using human-readable domain names instead of numerical IP addresses. DNS operates as a distributed hierarchical system of servers that store and distribute domain name information, allowing clients to resolve domain names to IP addresses and locate the corresponding servers on the Internet. DNS uses both UDP and TCP for communication, with UDP typically used for standard queries and TCP used for zone transfers and large responses. Furthermore, the Secure Shell (SSH) protocol is a secure network protocol used for remote access, administration, and secure file transfer over untrusted networks such as the Internet. SSH provides encrypted communication between client and server, protecting against eavesdropping, tampering, and session hijacking by encrypting data transmitted over the network. SSH operates on TCP port 22 and is widely used for securely accessing remote servers, managing network devices, and transferring files securely. Additionally, the Simple Mail Transfer Protocol (SMTP) is a network protocol used for transmitting email messages between email servers over the Internet. SMTP defines how email clients and servers communicate by exchanging email messages, sender and recipient addresses, and message metadata using a simple text-based protocol. SMTP operates on TCP port 25 and is widely used for sending and receiving email messages across different email systems and networks. Moreover, the File Transfer Protocol (FTP) is a network protocol used for transferring files between a client and a server over a network such as the Internet. FTP defines how files are transferred, listed, and managed on remote servers using a client-server architecture, with separate control and data connections established between client and server for issuing commands and transferring data. FTP operates on TCP ports 20 and 21 for data transfer and control, respectively, and is commonly used for uploading, downloading, and managing files on remote servers. Additionally, the Border Gateway

Protocol (BGP) is a critical network protocol used for routing and exchanging routing information between autonomous systems (AS) on the Internet. BGP defines how routers communicate and make routing decisions by exchanging routing updates, network reachability information, and policy attributes to determine the best path for forwarding packets to their destination. BGP operates on TCP port 179 and is essential for ensuring the stability, scalability, and security of the global Internet routing infrastructure. Furthermore, the Internet Control Message Protocol (ICMP) is a network protocol used for diagnostic and control purposes, such as error reporting, network testing, and troubleshooting. ICMP defines how network devices communicate by exchanging control messages, such as echo requests and replies (ping), destination unreachable, time exceeded, and parameter problems, to detect and report network errors and anomalies. ICMP operates at the network layer and is commonly used for testing network connectivity, measuring round-trip times, and diagnosing network issues. In summary, a deep dive into common network protocols provides valuable insights into how data is transmitted, received, and processed across computer networks, enabling organizations to design, deploy, and secure their network infrastructure effectively. By understanding the characteristics, functionalities, and vulnerabilities of common network protocols, organizations can implement robust security measures, monitor network traffic effectively, and mitigate security risks to protect their assets and data from cyber threats. Protocol fuzzing and exploitation represent critical techniques in the realm of cybersecurity, allowing researchers and practitioners to identify vulnerabilities and weaknesses in network protocols and applications, ultimately strengthening the security posture of systems and networks. One of the primary techniques employed in protocol fuzzing is the generation and injection of malformed or unexpected data packets into network protocols or applications to trigger unexpected behavior or crashes. Fuzzing tools such as American Fuzzy Lop (AFL), Peach Fuzzer, or Sulley can be used to automate the process of generating and sending malformed input to target protocols or applications, enabling researchers to identify vulnerabilities and potential attack vectors systematically. By fuzzing network protocols and applications, researchers can uncover memory corruption errors, buffer overflows, input validation flaws, or other security vulnerabilities that may lead to denial-of-service

(DoS) attacks, remote code execution (RCE), or privilege escalation. Moreover, protocol fuzzing can be performed using different fuzzing strategies or techniques, including random mutation-based fuzzing, dictionary-based fuzzing, or model-based fuzzing, each of which has its strengths and limitations. Random mutation-based fuzzing involves randomly modifying input data packets by flipping bits, changing bytes, or inserting random values to create diverse input variations and explore different code paths within the target application or protocol. Tools like AFL or libFuzzer implement random mutation-based fuzzing techniques by continuously mutating input data and monitoring the application's behavior for crashes or anomalies. Additionally, dictionary-based fuzzing involves using predefined or custom dictionaries of valid input values to guide the fuzzing process and generate semantically meaningful test cases that are more likely to trigger specific code paths or vulnerabilities within the target application or protocol. Dictionary-based fuzzing tools such as Peach Fuzzer or BooFuzz enable researchers to specify input templates, data types, and constraints to generate targeted test cases that exercise specific features or functionalities of the target application or protocol. Furthermore, model-based fuzzing involves building formal models or specifications of the target application or protocol's behavior and using them to generate valid and invalid input data that conforms to the expected protocol syntax and semantics. Model-based fuzzing tools like SAGE or LangFuzz leverage formal methods, symbolic execution, or constraint solving techniques to analyze protocol specifications, generate test cases, and explore different execution paths systematically, enabling researchers to uncover complex vulnerabilities or logic errors that may be missed by traditional fuzzing approaches. Additionally, protocol exploitation involves exploiting vulnerabilities discovered through fuzzing or other means to achieve unauthorized access, privilege escalation, or remote code execution on target systems or networks. One common technique used in protocol exploitation is crafting and sending specially crafted exploit payloads to exploit vulnerable network protocols or applications and gain control over target systems. Exploitation frameworks such as Metasploit or Core Impact provide a wide range of pre-built exploits, payloads, and post-exploitation modules that can be used to exploit known vulnerabilities in network protocols, services, or applications, enabling attackers to compromise target systems and achieve their objectives. Furthermore, protocol exploitation may involve chaining multiple vulnerabilities or attack techniques together to bypass security controls, evade detection, or escalate privileges on target systems effectively. Attackers may leverage techniques such as stack smashing, heap spraying, or return-oriented programming (ROP) to exploit memory corruption vulnerabilities, execute arbitrary code, or hijack control flow within target applications or protocols, enabling them to take full control of compromised systems or networks. Moreover, protocol exploitation often involves reverse engineering and analyzing vulnerable network protocols or applications to understand their internal workings, identify exploitable vulnerabilities, and develop reliable exploit code that can be used to compromise target systems in a controlled manner. Tools like IDA Pro, Ghidra, or Binary Ninja can be used to disassemble, debug, and analyze binary executables or network protocol implementations, enabling researchers to identify vulnerabilities, understand their root causes, and develop proof-of-concept (PoC) exploits that demonstrate the impact of the vulnerabilities. Additionally, protocol exploitation may involve the development and deployment of defensive measures and mitigations to protect against known vulnerabilities and prevent exploitation by attackers. Organizations can implement security best practices such as input validation, boundary checking, and memory protections to mitigate common vulnerabilities like buffer overflows, integer overflows, or format string vulnerabilities in network protocols or applications. Furthermore, organizations can deploy intrusion detection and prevention systems (IDS/IPS), firewalls, or network segmentation to monitor network traffic, detect anomalous behavior, and block malicious activities associated with protocol exploitation attempts. Moreover, organizations can apply patches, updates, or security fixes provided by vendors to address known vulnerabilities and mitigate the risk of exploitation by attackers. By staying vigilant, adopting a proactive security stance, and leveraging a combination of preventive, detective, and corrective controls, organizations can defend against protocol fuzzing and exploitation attempts effectively and minimize the impact of security incidents on their systems and networks.

Chapter 3: Cryptography and Cryptanalysis

Advanced encryption algorithms and techniques play a pivotal role in modern cybersecurity, safeguarding sensitive information and communications from unauthorized access, interception, or tampering, thereby ensuring confidentiality, integrity, and authenticity. One of the most widely used encryption algorithms is the Advanced Encryption Standard (AES), which is a symmetric encryption algorithm adopted by governments, organizations, and industries worldwide for securing data at rest and in transit. AES operates on fixed-size blocks of data (128, 192, or 256 bits) and uses a symmetric key to encrypt and decrypt plaintext, providing strong security guarantees against brute-force and cryptanalytic attacks. AES encryption can be performed using cryptographic libraries or command-line tools such as OpenSSL, which supports AES encryption and decryption with different key sizes and modes of operation. For example, to encrypt a file using AES-256 in CBC (Cipher Block Chaining) mode with OpenSSL, the following command can be used: openssl enc -aes-256-cbc -in plaintext.txt -out ciphertext.enc -k

<encryption_key>. Additionally, asymmetric encryption algorithms such as RSA (Rivest-Shamir-Adleman) play a crucial role in securing communication channels, digital signatures, and key exchange mechanisms in modern cryptography. RSA relies on the mathematical properties of large prime numbers to generate public and private key pairs, enabling secure encryption and decryption of messages between communicating parties. RSA encryption and decryption can be performed using cryptographic libraries or command-line tools such as OpenSSL. For example, to generate an RSA key pair with OpenSSL, the following commands can be used: openssl genpkey -algorithm RSA -out private_key.pem -aes256 (to generate a private key) and openssl rsa -pubout -in private_key.pem -out public_key.pem (to derive the corresponding public key). Moreover, elliptic curve cryptography (ECC) represents another class of asymmetric encryption algorithms that offer strong security guarantees with smaller key sizes compared to traditional algorithms like RSA. ECC relies on the mathematical properties of elliptic curves to generate public and private key pairs, enabling efficient encryption, decryption, and digital signatures with reduced computational overhead. ECC encryption and decryption can be performed

using cryptographic libraries or command-line tools such as OpenSSL. For example, to generate an ECC key pair with OpenSSL, the following commands can be used: openssl ecparam -name secp256k1 -genkey -noout -out private_key.pem (to generate a private key) and openssl ec -in private_key.pem -pubout -out public_key.pem (to derive the corresponding public key). Additionally, hash functions play a critical role in modern cryptography by providing data integrity and authentication through the generation of fixed-size, unique message digests or hash values from arbitrary input data. Commonly used hash functions include SHA-256 (Secure Hash Algorithm 256-bit) and SHA-3 (Secure Hash Algorithm 3), which generate 256-bit and 512-bit hash values, respectively. Hashing can be performed using cryptographic libraries or command-line tools such as OpenSSL. For example, to calculate the SHA-256 hash of a file with OpenSSL, the following command can be used: openssl dgst -sha256 <file>. Furthermore, cryptographic hashing techniques such as HMAC (Hash-based Message Authentication Code) provide additional security features by combining cryptographic hash functions with a secret key to generate message authentication codes that can verify the integrity and authenticity of transmitted data. HMAC can be implemented using cryptographic libraries or command-line tools such as OpenSSL. For example, to calculate the HMAC-SHA256 authentication code of a message with a secret key using OpenSSL, the following command can be used: echo -n "message" | openssl dgst -sha256 -hmac "<secret_key>". Moreover, key derivation functions (KDFs) are essential cryptographic techniques used to derive cryptographic keys from input data or passwords, enabling secure key generation and management in cryptographic applications. Commonly used KDFs include PBKDF2 (Password-Based Key Derivation Function 2) and HKDF (HMAC-based Extract-and-Expand Key Derivation Function), which provide secure key derivation with resistance to brute-force and dictionary attacks. KDFs can be implemented using cryptographic libraries or command-line tools such as OpenSSL. For example, to derive a cryptographic key from a password using PBKDF2 with OpenSSL, the following command can be used: openssl passwd -6 -salt <salt> -in <password>. Additionally, authenticated encryption algorithms such as AES-GCM (Galois/Counter Mode) and ChaCha20-Poly1305 provide combined confidentiality, integrity, and authenticity protection for transmitted data by encrypting messages and appending message authentication codes (MACs) to detect tampering or unauthorized modifications. Authenticated encryption can be performed using cryptographic libraries or command-line tools such as OpenSSL. For example, to encrypt and authenticate a message with AES-GCM using OpenSSL, the following command can be used: openssl enc -aes-256-gcm -in plaintext.txt -out ciphertext.enc -k <encryption_key>. Furthermore, quantum-resistant encryption algorithms represent an emerging area of research in cryptography aimed at developing cryptographic primitives and protocols that are resilient to attacks from quantum computers, which pose a significant threat to traditional encryption schemes such as RSA and ECC. Quantum-resistant encryption algorithms such as lattice-based cryptography, hash-based cryptography, and code-based cryptography offer promising solutions for securing communications in a post-quantum world. Quantum-resistant encryption algorithms can be implemented using cryptographic libraries or command-line tools such as OpenSSL, although their adoption and deployment are still in the early stages of development and standardization. In summary, advanced encryption algorithms and techniques play a critical role in modern cybersecurity by providing strong security guarantees for protecting sensitive information and communications against unauthorized access, interception, or tampering. By leveraging symmetric and asymmetric encryption algorithms, hash functions, HMAC, KDFs, authenticated encryption, and quantum-resistant cryptography, organizations can establish secure communication channels, encrypt data at rest and in transit, and mitigate the risks of data breaches, cyber attacks, and unauthorized disclosures.

Cryptanalysis methods represent a cornerstone in the field of cryptography, focusing on the analysis and breaking of cryptographic algorithms and systems to uncover weaknesses, vulnerabilities, or exploit opportunities, thereby compromising the security of encrypted data and communications. One of the most fundamental cryptanalysis techniques is brute-force attack, which involves systematically trying all possible keys or combinations until the correct key is found, enabling attackers to decrypt encrypted data or messages. Brute-force attacks can be deployed against symmetric and asymmetric encryption algorithms alike, although their effectiveness depends on the key size, complexity, and strength of the encryption algorithm. For example, to perform a brute-force attack against an encrypted file using a specific encryption algorithm, attackers can use tools such as John the Ripper or Hashcat, specifying the encryption algorithm, ciphertext, and potential key space to search for the correct key. Additionally, frequency analysis represents another classical cryptanalysis technique used to break encryption systems, particularly those based on substitution ciphers such as the Caesar cipher or the Vigenère cipher, which replace plaintext characters with different ciphertext characters based on predefined rules or tables. Frequency analysis relies on the statistical properties of natural languages, such as the frequency distribution of letters, digraphs, or trigraphs, to identify patterns, repetitions, or anomalies in the ciphertext that can be exploited to deduce the underlying plaintext. For example, to perform frequency analysis on a ciphertext encrypted with a simple substitution cipher, attackers can analyze the frequency distribution of letters or character pairs, identifying common patterns or correlations that may reveal the encryption key or plaintext message. Moreover, known plaintext attacks represent a powerful cryptanalysis technique that exploits the availability of plaintext-ciphertext pairs to deduce the encryption key or algorithm used to encrypt the data, enabling attackers to decrypt additional ciphertexts encrypted with the same key or algorithm. Known plaintext attacks are particularly effective against older encryption systems or protocols that lack proper key management, randomization, or padding mechanisms, allowing attackers to recover the encryption key through statistical analysis, algebraic manipulation, or cryptanalytic techniques. For example, to perform a known plaintext attack against an encrypted communication channel, attackers can intercept and analyze plaintext-ciphertext pairs exchanged between communicating parties, identifying patterns, similarities, or redundancies that may reveal information about the encryption key or algorithm. Additionally, chosen plaintext attacks represent an advanced cryptanalysis technique that leverages the ability to submit arbitrary plaintexts to an encryption system and observe the corresponding ciphertexts, enabling attackers to deduce information about the encryption key, algorithm, or internal state of the system. Chosen plaintext attacks are particularly effective against encryption systems or protocols that lack proper input validation, authentication, or integrity checks, allowing attackers to manipulate plaintext inputs and analyze the corresponding ciphertext outputs to gain insights into the encryption process. For example, to perform a chosen plaintext attack against a cryptographic system, attackers can submit carefully crafted plaintexts to the system and observe the resulting ciphertexts, analyzing patterns, correlations, or vulnerabilities that may reveal information about the encryption key or algorithm. Moreover, differential cryptanalysis represents a sophisticated cryptanalysis technique that exploits the differential behavior of encryption algorithms or cryptographic primitives to deduce information about the encryption key, algorithm, or internal state of the system, enabling attackers to break the encryption with reduced computational effort or complexity. Differential cryptanalysis relies on the analysis of plaintext-ciphertext pairs and the computation of statistical differentials or probabilities associated with specific input differences, enabling attackers to infer information about the encryption process and recover the encryption key or plaintext message. For example, to perform a differential cryptanalysis attack against an encryption algorithm, attackers can analyze the differential properties of the algorithm, identifying input-output pairs that exhibit specific differences or patterns that can be exploited to recover information about the encryption key or plaintext message. Additionally, algebraic cryptanalysis represents a powerful cryptanalysis technique that leverages algebraic techniques, mathematical structures, or symbolic manipulation to analyze the underlying mathematical properties of encryption algorithms or cryptographic primitives, enabling attackers to deduce information about the encryption key, algorithm, or internal state of the system, thereby breaking the encryption with reduced computational effort or complexity. Algebraic cryptanalysis is particularly effective against encryption algorithms or cryptographic primitives that can be represented and manipulated using algebraic equations or mathematical operations, allowing attackers to formulate and solve equations to recover the encryption key or plaintext message. For example, to perform an algebraic cryptanalysis attack against an encryption algorithm, attackers can model the algorithm as a system of algebraic equations, identifying relationships, dependencies, or constraints that can be exploited to recover information about the encryption key or plaintext message. Moreover, side-channel attacks represent a class of cryptanalysis techniques that exploit unintentional information leakage or observable physical properties of cryptographic implementations, such as timing, power consumption, electromagnetic emanations, or acoustic emissions, to deduce information about the encryption key, algorithm, or internal state of the system, enabling attackers to break the encryption with minimal computational resources or expertise. Side-channel attacks are particularly effective against real-world cryptographic systems or implementations that may exhibit vulnerabilities or weaknesses due to implementation flaws, hardware/software interactions, or environmental factors, allowing attackers to exploit observable characteristics or behaviors to recover sensitive information about the encryption process. For example, to perform a timing side-channel attack against a cryptographic implementation, attackers can measure the time taken to execute different cryptographic operations or algorithms, identifying variations, discrepancies, or patterns that may reveal information about the encryption key or algorithm.

Chapter 4: Advanced Exploitation Techniques

Memory corruption exploits represent a significant threat to the security of software systems and applications, allowing attackers to gain unauthorized access, execute arbitrary code, or achieve remote code execution on target systems by exploiting vulnerabilities in memory-handling mechanisms or memory safety checks. One of the most common types of memory corruption exploits is the buffer overflow, which occurs when an attacker writes data beyond the boundaries of a buffer allocated in memory, overwriting adjacent memory regions, such as stack variables, return addresses, or function pointers, and potentially altering the program's control flow or behavior. Buffer overflow vulnerabilities can be exploited using various techniques, including stack smashing, heap spraying, or return-oriented programming (ROP), each of which leverages different memory corruption primitives and attack vectors to achieve code execution or privilege escalation on target systems. For example, to exploit a buffer overflow vulnerability in a vulnerable C program, attackers can craft a malicious input string that exceeds the buffer's size, causing a stack-based buffer overflow and overwriting the return address with a controlled value that points to the attacker's shellcode or payload, enabling them to gain control of the program's execution flow. Additionally, heap-based buffer overflows represent another class of memory corruption exploits that occur when an attacker corrupts dynamically allocated memory regions, such as heap buffers or data structures, by writing data beyond their boundaries, leading to memory corruption, data leakage, or program crashes. Heap-based buffer overflow vulnerabilities can be exploited using techniques such as heap spraying, memory grooming, or heap metadata manipulation, each of which exploits different memory management primitives or data structures to achieve arbitrary memory read/write operations or code execution on target systems. For example, to exploit a heap-based buffer overflow vulnerability in a vulnerable application, attackers can craft specially crafted input data that triggers heap memory corruption, leading to heap metadata corruption, double free, or use-after-free conditions, enabling them to manipulate the program's memory layout and gain control of its execution flow. Moreover, format string vulnerabilities represent a type of memory corruption exploit that occurs when an attacker can control the format string parameter passed to a vulnerable function, such as printf() or sprintf(), allowing them to read or write arbitrary memory locations, leak sensitive information, or execute arbitrary code on target systems. Format string vulnerabilities can be exploited using techniques such as format string injection, format string exploitation, or format string manipulation, each of which leverages the format string parameter's properties to achieve memory corruption or code execution. For example, to exploit a format string vulnerability in a vulnerable C program, attackers can craft a specially formatted string that contains format specifiers and payload data, causing the vulnerable function to interpret the payload data as format specifiers and leak sensitive information or manipulate memory contents. Additionally, integer overflow vulnerabilities represent another class of memory corruption exploits that occur when an attacker manipulates arithmetic operations involving integers to produce unexpected results, such as wrapping, truncation, or overflow, leading to memory corruption, data leakage, or program crashes. Integer overflow vulnerabilities can be exploited using techniques such as integer overflow exploitation, integer truncation, or integer wrapping, each of which exploits arithmetic operations or type conversions to manipulate memory contents or control program behavior. For example, to exploit an integer overflow vulnerability in a vulnerable application, attackers can craft input data that triggers integer overflow during arithmetic operations, leading to unexpected results, memory corruption, or code execution on target systems. Moreover, stack canaries represent a mitigation technique used to detect and prevent buffer overflow attacks by placing a random value or "canary" between the buffer and the control data on the stack and checking its integrity before returning from the function, thereby detecting buffer overflows that overwrite the canary value and preventing code execution. Stack canaries can be implemented using compiler flags or runtime libraries such as StackGuard, ProPolice, or Microsoft Visual C++'s /GS flag, which insert code to check the canary value's integrity before returning from functions vulnerable to buffer overflow attacks. For example, to compile a C program with stack canaries enabled using GCC, the following command can be used: gcc -fstack-protector -o program program.c. Additionally, address space layout randomization (ASLR) represents another mitigation technique used to prevent memory corruption exploits by randomizing the memory layout of processes, such as the base addresses of executable code, stack, heap, and libraries, making it difficult for attackers to predict or manipulate memory addresses and execute arbitrary code. ASLR can be enabled using operating system-level protections or compiler flags such as -fPIE (position-independent executable) or -Wl,-z,relro,-z,now (relro and noexecstack) to randomize the memory layout of compiled binaries and libraries, making them less susceptible to memory corruption exploits. For example, to compile a position-independent executable (PIE) with ASLR enabled using GCC, the following command can be used: gcc -fPIE -pie -o program program.c. Return-Oriented Programming (ROP) exploits represent a sophisticated technique used by attackers to bypass modern memory protection mechanisms, such as Data Execution Prevention (DEP) and Address Space Layout Randomization (ASLR), by chaining together short code snippets called "gadgets" from the existing executable code within a process's address space to perform arbitrary computations or execute malicious payloads. The fundamental idea behind ROP exploits is to leverage existing code fragments or sequences of instructions, typically ending in a return instruction, to construct a malicious control flow graph that achieves the attacker's objectives without introducing new code into memory, thereby evading traditional security defenses and exploit mitigations. ROP exploits rely on the concept of "gadgets," which are short sequences of machine instructions ending in a return instruction (ret), allowing attackers to chain together multiple gadgets to construct arbitrary code execution paths and achieve their malicious goals. Gadgets can be found within the executable code, shared libraries, or dynamically loaded modules of a vulnerable process and typically consist of a sequence of instructions that manipulate the process's memory, registers, or control flow in predictable and controllable ways. For example, to identify potential ROP gadgets within a binary executable file, attackers can use tools such as ROPgadget, which analyzes the binary's code sections and identifies sequences of instructions that end in a return instruction, providing a list of potential gadgets that can be used to construct ROP chains. Once a set of suitable gadgets has been identified, attackers can construct a ROP chain by arranging the gadgets in a specific order and manipulating the process's stack or registers to redirect the control flow to the desired gadgets, achieving arbitrary code execution or privilege escalation. The construction of a ROP chain typically involves carefully crafting the stack layout or register values to control the execution flow of the program and execute the desired sequence of gadgets to achieve the attacker's objectives, such as spawning a shell, disabling security mechanisms, or escalating privileges. For example, to construct a ROP chain to bypass DEP and execute arbitrary code within a vulnerable process, attackers can use tools such as Ropper or ROPgadget to search for suitable gadgets and generate ROP chains that achieve their objectives, specifying the target architecture, binary file, and desired payload. Once the ROP chain has been constructed, attackers can trigger the vulnerability in the target process, such as a buffer overflow or format string vulnerability, and redirect the control flow to the ROP chain's entry point, causing the gadgets to be executed sequentially and achieving the desired outcome, such as executing a shellcode or injecting malicious code into the process's memory. Despite its complexity, ROP exploitation remains a prevalent technique used by attackers to bypass modern security defenses and exploit memory corruption vulnerabilities in software systems and applications, highlighting the importance of proactive security measures such as code auditing, vulnerability patching, and exploit mitigation techniques to mitigate the risk of ROP-based attacks. Additionally, the development of advanced security mechanisms such as Control Flow Integrity (CFI) and Code Randomization techniques aims to thwart ROP exploits by enforcing stricter control over the program's control flow and randomizing the location of code and data in memory, making it more difficult for attackers to construct ROP chains and execute arbitrary code. However, ROP exploitation continues to evolve as attackers adapt to new defensive measures and exploit mitigation techniques, underscoring the ongoing arms race between attackers and defenders in the field of cybersecurity.

Chapter 5: Post-Exploitation and Privilege Escalation

Escalating privileges on Windows systems represents a crucial aspect of penetration testing and security assessments, enabling testers to assess the security posture of Windows environments and identify vulnerabilities or misconfigurations that could be exploited by attackers to gain unauthorized access, elevate privileges, or escalate their control over compromised systems. One common technique for escalating privileges on Windows systems involves exploiting misconfigured permissions, insecure services, or unpatched vulnerabilities to gain access to sensitive system resources, such as files, directories, or registry keys, that grant elevated privileges or administrative access. For example, attackers can leverage tools like PowerUp, which is a PowerShell script designed to enumerate and exploit common Windows privilege escalation vulnerabilities, to identify misconfigured permissions, vulnerable services, or weak registry settings that can be exploited to escalate privileges on target systems. Additionally, exploiting vulnerable or misconfigured services running with elevated privileges represents another common method for escalating privileges on Windows systems, as many Windows services run with system-level privileges or have access to sensitive resources that can be abused by attackers to gain elevated privileges or execute arbitrary code. For instance, attackers can use tools like Metasploit, which is an open-source penetration testing framework, to exploit known vulnerabilities in Windows services, such as the Windows Print Spooler service, to execute arbitrary code with system-level privileges and escalate their access on compromised systems. Moreover, exploiting weak or misconfigured user credentials represents another prevalent technique for escalating privileges on Windows systems, as attackers can leverage stolen or brute-forced credentials to impersonate legitimate users, escalate their privileges, or gain access to sensitive resources that are only accessible to privileged accounts. To escalate privileges using compromised credentials, attackers can use techniques such as Pass-the-Hash (PtH) or Pass-the-Ticket (PtT) attacks, which involve extracting password hashes or Kerberos tickets from compromised systems and using them to authenticate and impersonate legitimate users, thereby gaining elevated privileges on target systems. Additionally, exploiting unpatched or zero-day vulnerabilities in Windows operating system components, drivers, or third-party software represents another effective method for escalating privileges on Windows systems, as attackers can exploit known vulnerabilities or develop custom exploits to bypass security mechanisms and gain elevated privileges on vulnerable systems. For example, attackers can use vulnerability scanning tools like Nessus or OpenVAS to identify missing patches or vulnerable software versions on target systems and exploit them using publicly available exploits or custom-developed payloads to escalate their privileges and gain full control over compromised systems. Furthermore, abusing built-in Windows features or functionalities to escalate privileges represents another tactic used by attackers to bypass security controls and gain elevated access on Windows systems, as many Windows features, such as scheduled tasks, services, or COM objects, run with elevated privileges or have access to sensitive resources that can be abused to escalate privileges or execute arbitrary code. For instance, attackers can use techniques like DLL hijacking, which involves placing a malicious DLL file in a directory searched by a vulnerable application or service, to load and execute arbitrary code with elevated privileges when the application or service is launched, thereby escalating their privileges on the target system. Additionally, leveraging Windows registry settings or Group Policy Objects (GPOs) to modify system configurations, permissions, or security policies represents another method for escalating privileges on Windows systems, as attackers can abuse misconfigured registry keys or GPO settings to grant themselves elevated privileges, bypass security controls, or disable security mechanisms that restrict their access to sensitive resources or system functions. For example, attackers can use tools like PowerSploit, which is a collection of PowerShell scripts, to manipulate Windows registry settings or GPOs to escalate their privileges, disable security features like Windows Defender or Windows Firewall, or enable remote access to compromised systems, thereby facilitating further exploitation or lateral movement within the target environment. Post-exploitation techniques for Linux systems play a crucial role in the lifecycle of a cyberattack, enabling attackers to maintain persistence, escalate privileges, exfiltrate data, and pivot to other systems within the target environment after gaining initial access to a Linux system. One common post-exploitation technique involves escalating privileges on compromised Linux systems, allowing attackers to obtain root or administrative access and perform actions that are restricted to privileged users, such as modifying system configurations, accessing sensitive files, or executing arbitrary commands with elevated privileges. To escalate privileges on Linux systems, attackers can leverage known vulnerabilities, misconfigured permissions, or insecure configurations to gain root access or exploit weak authentication mechanisms, such as sudo misconfigurations or vulnerable setuid binaries, to escalate privileges and execute arbitrary commands as root. For instance, attackers can use the sudo command with the -l option to list the sudo privileges associated with their current user account, identifying misconfigured sudo rules that grant them unrestricted access to specific commands or binaries, which can be abused to escalate privileges and execute malicious actions with root privileges. Additionally, exploiting kernel vulnerabilities or misconfigured kernel parameters represents another technique for escalating privileges on Linux systems, as attackers can exploit vulnerabilities in the Linux kernel or manipulate kernel parameters to gain elevated privileges or execute arbitrary code in kernel space. For example, attackers can use tools like DirtyCow or CVE-2016-5195 to exploit privilege escalation vulnerabilities in the Linux kernel, gaining root access and executing arbitrary code with kernel-level privileges on vulnerable systems. Moreover, leveraging misconfigured cron jobs or systemd timers represents another post-exploitation technique for maintaining persistence and executing arbitrary commands on Linux systems, as attackers can abuse scheduled tasks to establish backdoors, maintain access, or execute malicious payloads at predefined intervals without raising suspicion. To leverage cron jobs for post-exploitation, attackers can use commands like crontab -l to list the scheduled tasks associated with the current user account, identifying misconfigured cron jobs that execute with elevated privileges or execute sensitive commands, which can be hijacked or modified to execute arbitrary code or establish persistent access on the compromised system. Additionally, abusing SSH keys or misconfigured SSH configurations represents another technique for maintaining persistence and accessing Linux systems post-exploitation, as attackers can use compromised SSH keys or misconfigured SSH settings to establish persistent access, escalate privileges, or pivot to other systems within the target environment. For example, attackers can use commands like ssh -i to specify a compromised SSH private key for authentication, allowing them to access remote Linux systems using the corresponding public key without requiring a password, thereby maintaining persistent access and evading detection. Furthermore, exfiltrating sensitive data from compromised Linux systems represents a critical post-exploitation activity for attackers seeking to steal valuable information, such as credentials, intellectual property, or personal data, for financial gain or espionage purposes. To exfiltrate data from Linux systems, attackers can use commands like scp or rsync to securely transfer files or directories from the compromised system to an external server under their control, bypassing network-based security controls and monitoring mechanisms. Additionally, leveraging network pivoting or lateral movement techniques represents another post-exploitation strategy for attackers seeking to expand their foothold within a target environment and compromise additional systems or network segments. For instance, attackers can use tools like proxychains or SSH tunneling to pivot through compromised Linux systems and access internal network resources, bypassing perimeter defenses and firewalls to reach sensitive systems or services that are not directly accessible from the external network. Moreover, maintaining stealth and avoiding detection represents a critical aspect of post-exploitation operations on Linux systems, as attackers must evade detection by security monitoring tools, intrusion detection systems (IDS), and antivirus solutions to remain undetected and achieve their objectives. To evade detection, attackers can use techniques like obfuscation, encryption, or polymorphism to disguise their malicious activities and payloads, making it difficult for security tools to detect or block their actions effectively. Additionally, attackers can leverage rootkit or kernel-level rootkits to hide their presence on compromised Linux systems, manipulating system calls, processes, or network connections to evade detection by security solutions and remain stealthy within the target environment.

Chapter 6: Evading Detection and Anti-Forensics

Bypassing antivirus software represents a significant challenge for attackers seeking to execute malicious payloads or maintain persistence on target systems without detection, as antivirus solutions play a crucial role in detecting and blocking known malware, suspicious files, or malicious activities based on predefined signatures, behavioral analysis, or heuristics. One common technique for bypassing antivirus software involves using obfuscation or encryption to disguise malicious payloads and evade signature-based detection mechanisms, as attackers can encrypt or encode their payloads using techniques such as Base64 encoding, XOR encryption, or polymorphic code generation to obfuscate their true intent and bypass antivirus signature detection. For example, attackers can use tools like msfvenom, which is part of the Metasploit Framework, to generate encrypted or obfuscated payloads for various platforms and file formats, allowing them to evade antivirus detection and execute malicious code on target systems. Additionally, leveraging fileless malware or memory-resident payloads represents another technique for bypassing antivirus software, as fileless attacks execute malicious code directly in memory without touching the disk, making them difficult for antivirus solutions to detect or block using traditional signature-based scanning techniques. To deploy fileless malware, attackers can use techniques such as reflective DLL injection, PowerShell scripting, or in-memory exploitation of vulnerable processes to inject and execute malicious code in the memory space of legitimate processes, evading detection by antivirus solutions that rely on file-based scanning to detect malicious activity. Furthermore, polymorphic or metamorphic malware represents another evasion technique used by attackers to bypass antivirus software, as polymorphic malware generates unique variants of itself with each infection, making it challenging for antivirus solutions to detect or block new variants based on predefined signatures or patterns. To create polymorphic malware, attackers can use automated tools or custom scripts to generate random mutations or permutations of the original malware code, producing new variants that have different byte sequences or hash values, thereby evading signature-based detection mechanisms used by antivirus solutions. Moreover, leveraging packers or crypters represents another evasion technique for bypassing antivirus software, as packers and crypters compress or encrypt malicious payloads to avoid detection by antivirus solutions that rely on static signature matching or pattern recognition to identify known malware. To use packers or crypters, attackers can use tools like UPX, Themida, or MPRESS to compress or encrypt their payloads before distribution, making it difficult for antivirus solutions to analyze or detect the malicious code hidden within the packed or encrypted file. Additionally, leveraging code injection or process hollowing techniques represents another evasion strategy for bypassing antivirus software, as attackers can inject malicious code into legitimate processes or replace benign code with malicious code within the memory space of running processes to evade detection by antivirus solutions that rely on file-based scanning or signature-based detection mechanisms. To perform code injection or process hollowing, attackers can use techniques such as DLL injection, process hollowing, or reflective loading to inject or execute malicious code within the context of legitimate processes, making it difficult for antivirus solutions to distinguish between legitimate and malicious activity. Furthermore, using rootkits or kernel-level malware represents an advanced evasion technique for bypassing antivirus software, as rootkits manipulate the operating system's kernel or low-level components to hide their presence and evade detection by antivirus solutions that operate at higher levels of the system stack. To deploy rootkits or kernel-level malware, attackers can use techniques such as rootkit installation, kernel hooking, or direct kernel object manipulation to modify system behavior, intercept system calls, or hide malicious activity from security solutions, making it difficult for antivirus solutions to detect or remove the rootkit from the compromised system. Additionally, leveraging social engineering or phishing attacks represents another evasion technique for bypassing antivirus software, as attackers can trick users into downloading and executing malicious files or payloads by disguising them as legitimate software updates, attachments, or links in phishing emails or malicious websites. To deploy social engineering or phishing attacks, attackers can use techniques such as email spoofing, fake websites, or enticing messages to deceive users into downloading and executing malicious files or payloads, bypassing antivirus solutions that rely on user awareness and behavior analysis to detect or block suspicious activity. Anti-forensic tools and techniques represent a significant challenge for digital investigators and forensic analysts tasked with examining digital evidence and reconstructing the timeline of events in cybercrime investigations, as these tools and techniques are specifically designed to obfuscate, manipulate, or destroy digital evidence to hinder or thwart forensic analysis and attribution efforts. One common anti-forensic technique involves data wiping or disk sanitization, where attackers use tools like dd or shred to overwrite sensitive files or disk partitions with random data multiple times, making it difficult or impossible for forensic tools to recover the original data or artifacts from the overwritten sectors. For example, attackers can use the dd command in Linux to overwrite a disk partition with random data, specifying parameters such as the input file (if=/dev/urandom), the output file (of=/dev/sdX), and the block size (bs=4k) to perform a secure wipe of the target disk partition, preventing data recovery attempts by forensic tools. Additionally, leveraging file deletion or hiding techniques represents another anti-forensic strategy used by attackers to conceal incriminating evidence or sensitive information from digital investigators, as attackers can use commands like rm or del to delete files or directories from the filesystem or hide them using techniques such as file system-level hiding or steganography. To delete files securely, attackers can use the rm command with the -rf option in Linux to recursively delete files and directories, ensuring that they are not recoverable by forensic tools, while hiding files or directories can involve techniques such as renaming them with a dot prefix (e.g., .hidden_file) or using file attributes to mark them as hidden. Moreover, exploiting forensic tool weaknesses or vulnerabilities represents another anti-forensic technique used by attackers to subvert or evade digital forensic analysis, as attackers can identify and exploit flaws in forensic tools, file formats, or operating system components to manipulate or corrupt digital evidence and undermine the integrity of forensic investigations. For example, attackers can craft malicious files or payloads that exploit vulnerabilities in forensic software or file parsers to cause buffer overflows, memory corruption, or denial-of-service (DoS) conditions, leading to data loss, system crashes, or manipulation of forensic artifacts. Furthermore, using encryption or steganography techniques represents another anti-forensic strategy for concealing sensitive information or incriminating evidence from digital investigators, as attackers can encrypt files or hide data within innocuous-looking files or multimedia content to evade detection and prevent unauthorized access. To encrypt files, attackers can use tools like GPG or OpenSSL to encrypt sensitive data using strong cryptographic algorithms and keys, making it unreadable without the decryption key, while steganography techniques involve embedding data within images, audio files, or other digital media using tools like Steghide or OpenStego, making it difficult for forensic tools to detect or recover the hidden information without knowledge of the steganographic technique used. Additionally, employing anti-forensic countermeasures or evasion tactics during cyber operations represents another strategy for adversaries seeking to cover their tracks and evade detection by forensic analysts, as attackers can use techniques such as VPNs, proxy servers, or anonymization networks to obfuscate their online activities and mask their digital footprint. For example, attackers can use Tor or I2P to anonymize their Internet traffic and conceal their IP addresses, making it challenging for forensic analysts to attribute malicious activities to specific individuals or organizations, while using virtual private networks (VPNs) or proxy servers can help attackers bypass network-based monitoring and logging systems, further complicating forensic analysis efforts. Moreover, manipulating system logs or event records represents another anti-forensic technique used by attackers to conceal their activities and erase traces of malicious behavior from compromised systems, as attackers can use commands like clear or del to delete log files or manipulate timestamps to alter the chronological order of events, making it difficult for forensic analysts to reconstruct the timeline of events or identify the root cause of security incidents.

Chapter 7: Red Team Operations

Planning and conducting red team engagements represent essential components of a comprehensive cybersecurity strategy aimed at evaluating an organization's defensive capabilities, identifying weaknesses, and improving overall security posture through realistic adversary simulations. Red team engagements involve the simulation of real-world cyber attacks by skilled professionals known as red teamers, who adopt the mindset, tactics, and techniques of malicious actors to assess an organization's resilience to sophisticated threats and uncover vulnerabilities that may go undetected by traditional security measures. One crucial aspect of planning red team engagements is defining the scope and objectives of the exercise, which involves determining the target systems, networks, applications, and personnel to be assessed, as well as specifying the goals, constraints, and rules of engagement to ensure that the exercise aligns with the organization's risk tolerance, compliance requirements, and strategic objectives. To define the scope and objectives of a red team engagement, organizations can use techniques such as threat modeling, risk assessment, and scenario planning to identify critical assets, high-value targets, and potential attack vectors that should be prioritized during the assessment. Additionally, establishing clear communication channels, reporting structures, and escalation procedures is essential for effective coordination and collaboration between the red team, blue team (defenders), and other stakeholders involved in the engagement, ensuring that findings, observations, and recommendations are communicated promptly and acted upon to improve defensive capabilities and mitigate identified risks. To facilitate communication and collaboration during red team engagements, organizations can use tools such as collaboration platforms, incident response frameworks, and threat intelligence sharing platforms to share information, coordinate actions, and track progress throughout the assessment lifecycle, enabling timely decision-making and response to emerging threats or incidents. Moreover, conducting thorough reconnaissance and intelligence gathering activities is critical for red teamers to gather information about the target environment, including network topology, system configurations, software versions, user behaviors, and security controls, which can be used to identify potential attack vectors, weaknesses, and blind spots that may be exploited during the engagement. To conduct reconnaissance and intelligence gathering, red teamers can use open-source intelligence (OSINT) techniques, automated scanning tools, and manual reconnaissance methods to collect information from publicly available sources, social media platforms, internet archives, and other sources of digital footprint data, providing insights into the organization's attack surface and potential avenues of exploitation. Furthermore, selecting appropriate attack techniques, tactics, and procedures (TTPs) is crucial for red teamers to simulate realistic threat scenarios and emulate the behavior of sophisticated adversaries, ensuring that the engagement provides meaningful insights into the organization's defensive capabilities and resilience to advanced cyber threats. To select attack techniques and TTPs, red teamers can leverage threat intelligence, penetration testing frameworks, and attack simulation platforms to identify relevant threats, vulnerabilities, and attack vectors that are likely to be encountered in the target environment, tailoring the engagement to simulate specific threat actors, scenarios, or attack chains that pose the greatest risk to the organization's security posture. Additionally, executing well-planned and coordinated attack sequences is essential for red teamers to achieve their objectives while minimizing the risk of disruption or unintended consequences, as the success of the engagement depends on the ability to navigate complex attack paths, evade detection, and achieve the desired impact without causing undue harm or disruption to business operations. To execute attack sequences, red teamers can use techniques such as privilege escalation, lateral movement, data exfiltration, and persistence mechanisms to simulate the various stages of a cyber attack, leveraging tools, tactics, and procedures that are commonly used by real-world adversaries to compromise target systems and achieve their objectives. Moreover, documenting and reporting findings, observations, and recommendations is critical for ensuring that the insights gained from the red team engagement are effectively communicated to stakeholders and actionable insights are provided to improve defensive capabilities and mitigate identified risks. To document and report findings, red teamers can use standardized reporting templates, incident response frameworks, and threat modeling methodologies to organize and communicate key findings, including details of observed vulnerabilities, weaknesses, and recommendations for remediation or mitigation, enabling stakeholders to prioritize and address security gaps effectively. Additionally, conducting post-engagement debriefings and lessons learned sessions is essential for capturing and disseminating knowledge, insights, and best practices gleaned from the red team engagement, enabling the organization to learn from the experience, refine defensive strategies, and enhance preparedness for future cyber threats and attacks. To conduct post-engagement debriefings and lessons learned sessions, organizations can use techniques such as tabletop exercises, scenario-based simulations, and interactive workshops to facilitate open discussion, knowledge sharing, and collaborative problem-solving among participants, fostering a culture of continuous improvement and resilience in the face of evolving cyber threats. Red team tactics, techniques, and procedures (TTPs) encompass a wide range of strategies, methods, and procedures employed by red teamers to simulate realistic cyber attacks and assess an organization's defensive capabilities, resilience, and preparedness against sophisticated adversaries. These TTPs are continually evolving and adapting to circumvent security controls, exploit vulnerabilities, and achieve the attacker's objectives, making them a crucial focus area for red team engagements and cybersecurity assessments. One common red team TTP involves reconnaissance and intelligence gathering, where red teamers collect information about the target environment, including network topology, system configurations, user behaviors, and security controls, to identify potential attack vectors, weaknesses, and blind spots that may be exploited during the engagement. To conduct reconnaissance and intelligence gathering, red teamers can use techniques such as open-source intelligence (OSINT), automated scanning tools, and manual reconnaissance methods to collect information from publicly available sources, social media platforms, internet archives, and other sources of digital footprint data, providing insights into the organization's attack surface and potential avenues of exploitation. Additionally, leveraging social engineering tactics represents another common TTP used by red teamers to manipulate human behavior, exploit trust relationships, and trick individuals into divulging sensitive information or performing actions that compromise security, such as clicking on malicious links, downloading malware-infected files, or disclosing credentials. To execute social engineering attacks, red teamers can use techniques such as phishing emails, pretexting calls, or physical infiltration to establish rapport with targets, gain their trust, and elicit the desired response, bypassing technical security controls and exploiting human vulnerabilities to achieve their objectives. Furthermore, leveraging insider threats or compromised accounts represents another TTP used by red teamers to gain unauthorized access to target systems, networks, or data, as attackers can exploit insider privileges, weak authentication mechanisms, or compromised credentials to bypass perimeter defenses and move laterally within the organization's infrastructure. To exploit insider threats or compromised accounts, red teamers can use techniques such as credential harvesting, password spraying, or privilege escalation to escalate their privileges, elevate their access levels, and maintain persistence on target systems, evading detection and surveillance by traditional security measures. Additionally, exploiting misconfigurations or vulnerabilities in target systems, applications, or infrastructure represents another common TTP used by red teamers to gain unauthorized access, execute arbitrary code, or achieve other malicious objectives, as attackers can leverage weaknesses in software, hardware, or network configurations to bypass security controls and compromise target assets. To exploit misconfigurations or vulnerabilities, red teamers can use techniques such as exploit development, vulnerability scanning, or penetration testing to identify and exploit weaknesses in target systems, applications, or services, gaining unauthorized access and achieving their objectives while evading detection by defenders. Moreover, using command and control (C2) infrastructure represents another critical TTP used by red teamers to establish communication channels, coordinate actions, and control compromised systems remotely, as attackers can deploy C2 servers, implants, or backdoors to maintain persistence, exfiltrate data, or execute commands on compromised hosts, evading detection and surveillance by defenders. To establish C2 infrastructure, red teamers can use techniques such as domain generation algorithms (DGA), encrypted communication protocols, or covert channels to disguise their activities and evade detection by network monitoring tools, intrusion detection systems (IDS), or security information and event management (SIEM) solutions. Additionally, employing lateral movement and privilege escalation techniques represents another essential TTP used by red teamers to expand their foothold within the target environment, escalate their privileges, and access sensitive resources or data, as attackers can use techniques such as pass-the-hash, pass-the-ticket, or remote code execution to move laterally between systems, compromise additional hosts, and achieve their objectives while evading detection by defenders. To execute lateral movement and privilege escalation, red teamers can use techniques such as PowerShell scripting, remote desktop protocol (RDP) sessions, or remote procedure calls (RPC) to access and manipulate target systems, escalate their privileges, and maintain persistence on compromised hosts, evading detection and surveillance by defenders.

Chapter 8: Exploiting Web Applications and APIs

Advanced SQL injection techniques represent sophisticated methods employed by attackers to exploit vulnerabilities in web applications and manipulate backend databases through SQL queries, allowing unauthorized access, data theft, or other malicious activities. These techniques leverage vulnerabilities in input validation mechanisms or inadequate security controls to inject malicious SQL code into application inputs, bypassing authentication mechanisms, executing arbitrary commands, or retrieving sensitive information from the database. One common advanced SQL injection technique is blind SQL injection, where attackers exploit blind spots in error messages, response times, or other observable behaviors to infer information about the database schema, table structures, or data contents indirectly, without receiving explicit error messages or responses from the application. To execute blind SQL injection attacks, attackers can use techniques such as boolean-based blind injection or time-based blind injection to construct SQL queries that elicit predictable responses from the database, allowing them to infer the presence of vulnerabilities, identify table names, column names, or data types, and extract sensitive information gradually through iterative probing and analysis. Another advanced SQL injection technique is out-of-band (OOB) SQL injection, where attackers leverage alternative communication channels, such as DNS or HTTP requests, to exfiltrate data from the database or interact with external systems indirectly, bypassing network-based detection or filtering mechanisms. To execute out-of-band SQL injection attacks, attackers can use techniques such as DNS exfiltration or HTTP-based callbacks to embed malicious payloads in SQL queries, trigger network requests to external servers controlled by the attacker, and receive responses containing extracted data or executing arbitrary commands, circumventing network-based security controls and evading detection by traditional monitoring solutions. Additionally, exploiting second-order SQL injection vulnerabilities represents another advanced technique used by attackers to manipulate data or execute arbitrary commands indirectly, as attackers inject malicious payloads into application inputs that are stored persistently in the database and executed at a later time or by a different user, allowing them to bypass input validation checks or security controls applied during the initial request. To exploit second-order SQL injection vulnerabilities, attackers can inject malicious payloads into user-generated content, metadata fields, or other inputs stored in the database, anticipating that the injected payloads will be retrieved and processed by the application at a later time, potentially in a different context or by a different user, enabling them to achieve their objectives while evading immediate detection or blocking by the application's defenses. Furthermore, leveraging advanced SQL injection techniques to escalate privileges, execute operating system commands, or achieve command execution on the underlying server represents another common tactic used by attackers to escalate their impact, expand their foothold, or achieve persistence in compromised environments, as attackers can use techniques such as stacked queries, function calls, or operating system commands to extend the scope of their attacks beyond the confines of the database and compromise the underlying infrastructure. To escalate privileges or execute operating system commands via SQL injection, attackers can use techniques such as stored procedure injection, command injection, or shell injection to execute arbitrary code or system commands on the underlying server, gaining unauthorized access, executing arbitrary code, or manipulating the system's configuration, bypassing application-level security controls and achieving their objectives while evading detection by traditional defensive measures. Additionally, leveraging advanced SQL injection techniques in conjunction with other attack vectors, such as cross-site scripting (XSS), file inclusion, or server-side request forgery (SSRF), represents another tactic used by attackers to orchestrate complex, multi-stage attacks that exploit multiple vulnerabilities or weaknesses in the target application or infrastructure, enabling them to achieve a higher level of compromise, persistence, or impact than would be possible with SQL injection alone. To orchestrate multi-stage attacks, attackers can use techniques such as SQL injection to bypass authentication mechanisms, escalate privileges, or retrieve sensitive information from the database, then use the obtained credentials, session tokens, or other artifacts to launch additional attacks against other components or services within the target environment, such as injecting malicious payloads into user-generated content to trigger XSS vulnerabilities, exploiting file inclusion vulnerabilities to execute arbitrary code on the server, or abusing SSRF vulnerabilities to access internal systems or resources indirectly, enabling them to achieve their objectives while evading detection or blocking by traditional security controls.

Exploiting RESTful APIs for remote code execution represents a significant threat to web applications and APIs, allowing attackers to execute arbitrary code on the server-side and compromise the integrity, confidentiality, and availability of the underlying systems and data. This technique leverages vulnerabilities in the design, implementation, or configuration of RESTful APIs to inject malicious payloads, bypass security controls, and execute commands or scripts remotely, enabling attackers to achieve unauthorized access, privilege escalation, or data exfiltration, among other malicious activities. One common method for exploiting RESTful APIs for remote code execution is injection attacks, where attackers manipulate input parameters, request headers, or data payloads to inject malicious code into API requests, exploiting vulnerabilities such as insufficient input validation, insecure deserialization, or improper handling of user-controlled data by the application. To execute injection attacks against RESTful APIs, attackers can use techniques such as SQL injection, XML injection, or command injection to inject malicious payloads into API requests, triggering the execution of arbitrary code or system commands on the server-side, bypassing authentication mechanisms, and gaining unauthorized access to sensitive resources or data. Additionally, exploiting insecure object references or broken access controls in RESTful APIs represents another common tactic used by attackers to gain unauthorized access to sensitive functionality or resources, as attackers can manipulate resource identifiers, authentication tokens, or session identifiers to access restricted endpoints, perform unauthorized actions, or escalate privileges within the application. To exploit insecure object references or broken access controls, attackers can use techniques such as parameter tampering, session fixation, or brute-force attacks to manipulate API requests, impersonate legitimate users, or escalate their privileges within the application, enabling them to bypass authorization checks, access sensitive data, or perform unauthorized actions without proper authentication or authorization. Furthermore, exploiting insecure deserialization vulnerabilities in RESTful APIs represents another significant risk, as attackers can manipulate serialized objects, data structures, or payloads to trigger unexpected behaviors or execute arbitrary code on the server-side, compromising the integrity, confidentiality, or availability of the underlying systems and data. To exploit insecure deserialization vulnerabilities, attackers can craft malicious payloads, such as serialized objects containing arbitrary code or system commands, and submit them to the target API, exploiting vulnerabilities in the deserialization process to execute arbitrary code or system commands on the server-side, bypassing security controls and gaining unauthorized access to sensitive resources or data. Moreover, exploiting misconfigured or vulnerable components in RESTful APIs, such as frameworks, libraries, or middleware, represents another common tactic used by attackers to achieve remote code execution, as attackers can identify and exploit weaknesses in the underlying infrastructure or dependencies to execute arbitrary code or system commands on the server-side, compromising the security and integrity of the application. To exploit misconfigured or vulnerable components in RESTful APIs, attackers can use techniques such as version enumeration, fingerprinting, or exploit chaining to identify known vulnerabilities or weaknesses in the target environment, then use publicly available exploits, proof-of-concept code, or custom scripts to exploit the identified vulnerabilities and achieve remote code execution on the server-side, bypassing security controls and gaining unauthorized access to sensitive resources or data. Additionally, leveraging insecure authentication mechanisms or session management in RESTful APIs represents another common tactic used by attackers to gain unauthorized access to sensitive functionality or resources, as attackers can exploit weaknesses such as weak passwords, session fixation, or session hijacking to impersonate legitimate users, escalate their privileges, or perform unauthorized actions within the application. To exploit insecure authentication mechanisms or session management, attackers can use techniques such as credential stuffing, session sniffing, or session replay attacks to capture or replay authentication tokens, impersonate legitimate users, or bypass authentication checks within the application, enabling them to gain unauthorized access to sensitive functionality or resources and perform malicious activities, including remote code execution.

Chapter 9: Advanced Wireless Attacks

Breaking WPA3 encryption, the latest iteration of Wi-Fi Protected Access, represents a significant challenge for attackers due to its enhanced security features and robust encryption algorithms designed to protect wireless communications from unauthorized access and eavesdropping. However, despite its improvements over previous versions, WPA3 is not immune to vulnerabilities, and attackers continue to explore techniques and exploits to circumvent its protections and compromise wireless networks. One method for breaking WPA3 encryption is through brute-force attacks, where attackers attempt to guess the passphrase or pre-shared key used to encrypt Wi-Fi communications by systematically trying every possible combination until the correct one is found. To conduct a brute-force attack against WPA3, attackers can use tools such as Aircrack-ng or Hashcat to generate and test potential passwords against captured handshake packets or offline data, exploiting weaknesses in password complexity, length, or entropy to increase the likelihood of success. Additionally, leveraging dictionary-based attacks represents another approach for breaking WPA3 encryption, where attackers use precompiled lists of commonly used passwords, phrases, or word combinations to guess the passphrase or pre-shared key associated with the target Wi-Fi network. To perform a dictionary attack against WPA3, attackers can use tools such as Crunch or John the Ripper to generate wordlists based on common patterns, themes, or character sets, then use these lists to systematically test potential passwords against captured handshake packets or offline data, exploiting predictable or insecure passphrase choices made by users. Furthermore, exploiting implementation flaws or vulnerabilities in WPA3-compatible devices or software represents another avenue for breaking WPA3 encryption, as attackers can identify and exploit weaknesses in the protocol implementation, key exchange mechanisms, or cryptographic algorithms to bypass security controls, intercept communications, or decrypt encrypted traffic. To exploit implementation flaws or vulnerabilities in WPA3, attackers can conduct security assessments, code reviews, or penetration tests to identify weaknesses or vulnerabilities in the target devices or software, then develop and deploy exploits, proof-of-concept code, or custom scripts to exploit the identified vulnerabilities and compromise the security of the wireless network. Moreover, leveraging side-channel attacks represents another technique for breaking WPA3 encryption, where attackers exploit unintended or unexpected behaviors in the physical implementation of cryptographic algorithms, key exchange protocols, or wireless communication protocols to extract sensitive information, such as encryption keys or authentication tokens, from the target system or device. To conduct a side-channel attack against WPA3, attackers can use techniques such as timing analysis, power analysis, or electromagnetic analysis to monitor and analyze the physical characteristics of the target device or system during cryptographic operations, then use this information to infer sensitive data, such as encryption keys or authentication tokens, and compromise the security of the wireless network. Additionally, exploiting weaknesses in the Wi-Fi Protected Setup (WPS) protocol, which is used to simplify the process of connecting devices to WPA3-protected networks, represents another avenue for breaking WPA3 encryption, as attackers can abuse vulnerabilities in the WPS implementation to bypass security controls, brute-force PINs, or gain unauthorized access to the network. To exploit WPS vulnerabilities, attackers can use tools such as Reaver or Bully to automate the process of brute-forcing WPS PINs, exploiting weaknesses in the protocol design or implementation to recover the passphrase or pre-shared key associated with the target Wi-Fi network, and compromise the security of the wireless network. Furthermore, leveraging weaknesses in the extensible authentication protocol (EAP) frameworks or authentication mechanisms used in WPA3 enterprise networks represents another tactic for breaking WPA3 encryption, as attackers can identify and exploit vulnerabilities in the EAP implementation, authentication protocols, or certificate management processes to bypass security controls, impersonate legitimate users, or intercept sensitive data exchanged during the authentication process. To exploit EAP vulnerabilities, attackers can conduct protocol analysis, traffic interception, or man-in-the-middle attacks to capture and manipulate authentication messages exchanged between the client and server, then use these messages to bypass authentication checks, impersonate legitimate users, or obtain sensitive information, compromising the security of the wireless network.

Wireless mesh network exploitation represents a

significant area of interest for both security researchers and attackers alike due to the proliferation of mesh network deployments in various environments, including smart cities, industrial IoT, and urban infrastructure, offering benefits such as increased coverage, scalability, and resilience, but also introducing new security challenges and attack vectors that must be addressed. One common method for exploiting wireless mesh networks is through unauthorized access, where attackers attempt to gain unauthorized entry into the network infrastructure, compromising the confidentiality, integrity, and availability of the network resources and communications. To gain unauthorized access to a wireless mesh network, attackers can use techniques such as wireless sniffing, packet capture, or rogue access point deployment to eavesdrop on network traffic, intercept sensitive information, or impersonate legitimate network nodes, exploiting vulnerabilities in the network protocols, authentication mechanisms, or encryption algorithms to bypass security controls and gain unauthorized access. Additionally, exploiting vulnerabilities in the mesh routing protocols represents another avenue for attackers to compromise the security of wireless mesh networks, as vulnerabilities in the routing protocols or routing algorithms used to establish and maintain network connections can be exploited to manipulate network traffic, redirect data flows, or disrupt network operations, compromising the availability, reliability, and performance of the network infrastructure. To exploit vulnerabilities in mesh routing protocols, attackers can conduct protocol analysis, traffic interception, or fuzzing attacks to identify weaknesses or implementation flaws in the routing protocols, then develop and deploy exploits, proof-of-concept code, or custom scripts to exploit the identified vulnerabilities and compromise the security of the network infrastructure. Moreover, leveraging weaknesses in the wireless mesh network infrastructure or deployment architecture represents another tactic for attackers to exploit wireless mesh networks, as vulnerabilities in the network hardware, firmware, or configuration settings can be exploited to gain unauthorized access, escalate privileges, or execute arbitrary code on the network devices, compromising the security and integrity of the network infrastructure. To exploit weaknesses in the wireless mesh network infrastructure, attackers can conduct vulnerability scanning, penetration testing, or reverse engineering to identify vulnerabilities or weaknesses in the network devices, then develop and deploy exploits, proof-of-concept code, or custom scripts to exploit the identified vulnerabilities and compromise the security of the network infrastructure. Furthermore, leveraging insider threats or compromised devices represents another tactic for attackers to exploit wireless mesh networks, as insider threats or compromised devices can be used to gain unauthorized access, exfiltrate sensitive information, or launch attacks against other network nodes, compromising the confidentiality, integrity, and availability of the network resources and communications. To leverage insider threats or compromised devices, attackers can conduct social engineering, phishing, or malware attacks to trick legitimate users into divulging their credentials or installing malicious software on their devices, then use these credentials or compromised devices to gain unauthorized access, escalate privileges, or execute arbitrary code on the network infrastructure, compromising the security and integrity of the network resources and communications. Additionally, exploiting weaknesses in the encryption mechanisms or security controls used to protect wireless mesh networks represents another tactic for attackers to compromise the security of wireless mesh networks, as vulnerabilities in the encryption algorithms, key management protocols, or authentication mechanisms used to secure network communications can be exploited to intercept, decrypt, or manipulate network traffic, compromising the confidentiality, integrity, and availability of the network resources and communications. To exploit weaknesses in the encryption mechanisms or security controls used to protect wireless mesh networks, attackers can conduct cryptographic analysis, protocol reverse engineering, or implementation attacks to identify vulnerabilities or weaknesses in the encryption algorithms, then develop and deploy exploits, proof-of-concept code, or custom scripts to exploit the identified vulnerabilities and compromise the security of the network infrastructure.

Chapter 10: Threat Hunting and Incident Response

Proactive threat hunting strategies play a crucial role in modern cybersecurity operations, aiming to detect and mitigate potential threats before they escalate into full-blown security incidents or breaches, emphasizing a proactive approach to identifying and neutralizing emerging threats, vulnerabilities, and attack vectors that may evade traditional security controls or remain undetected by automated security solutions. One proactive threat hunting technique involves leveraging threat intelligence feeds and indicators of compromise (IOCs) to identify suspicious activities, behaviors, or patterns that may indicate the presence of malicious actors or malicious activities within the network environment, using tools such as OpenIOC or MISP to collect, analyze, and correlate threat intelligence data from various sources, including commercial feeds, open-source repositories, or internal security logs, then using this information to proactively search for signs of compromise or indicators of malicious activity within the network infrastructure. Another proactive threat hunting strategy involves conducting regular vulnerability assessments and penetration tests to identify and remediate weaknesses, vulnerabilities, or misconfigurations in the network infrastructure, applications, or systems, using tools such as Nessus or Metasploit to scan for known vulnerabilities, assess the security posture of network assets, and simulate real-world attack scenarios to identify potential entry points, attack vectors, or exploitation opportunities that could be leveraged by adversaries to compromise the security of the organization. Moreover, leveraging behavior-based anomaly detection techniques represents another proactive threat hunting approach, where security analysts monitor network traffic, user behavior, or system activity for deviations from normal patterns or baseline behaviors that may indicate the presence of anomalous or malicious activities, using tools such as Splunk or ELK Stack to collect, analyze, and visualize log data, network telemetry, or security events in real-time, then using machine learning algorithms or statistical analysis to identify suspicious anomalies or outliers that warrant further investigation or response from the security team. Additionally, conducting endpoint forensics and memory analysis represents another proactive threat hunting tactic, where security analysts analyze the forensic artifacts, memory dumps, or system logs collected from endpoint devices to identify signs of compromise, persistence mechanisms, or post-exploitation activities that may indicate the presence of advanced threats or stealthy adversaries within the network environment, using tools such as Volatility or Autopsy to analyze memory images, disk forensics, or system logs for indicators of compromise (IOCs), anomalous behavior, or malicious activities that may require further investigation or response from the incident response team. Furthermore, leveraging network traffic analysis and packet inspection techniques represents another proactive threat hunting strategy, where security analysts monitor and analyze network traffic, protocol behavior, or packet payloads for signs of malicious activity, command-and-control (C2) communications, or data exfiltration attempts, using tools such as Wireshark or Zeek to capture, decode, and analyze network packets, then using intrusion detection systems (IDS) or network intrusion prevention systems (IPS) to detect and block suspicious traffic patterns or malicious behaviors that may indicate the presence of an active threat or ongoing attack within the network environment. Additionally, leveraging threat hunting platforms and automation tools represents another proactive approach to threat hunting, where security analysts use specialized platforms or automated workflows to streamline and accelerate the threat hunting process, using tools such as Elastic Security or CyberArk to centralize, automate, and orchestrate threat hunting activities, including data collection, analysis, and response, then using custom scripts or playbooks to automate repetitive tasks, correlate security events, or prioritize alerts based on risk factors or severity levels, enabling security teams to proactively identify and mitigate potential threats in a timely and efficient manner. Moreover, establishing a threat hunting framework or playbook represents another proactive approach to threat hunting, where security teams develop standardized methodologies, procedures, and best practices for conducting threat hunting activities, using tools such as MITRE ATT&CK or NIST Cybersecurity Framework to define threat hunting objectives, prioritize threat vectors, and align threat hunting activities with organizational goals and risk tolerance, then using predefined workflows, checklists, or decision trees to guide security analysts through the threat hunting process, ensuring consistency, repeatability, and effectiveness in identifying and mitigating potential threats within the network environment. Additionally, fostering a culture of collaboration and knowledge sharing represents another key aspect of proactive threat hunting, where security teams collaborate with internal stakeholders, external partners, or industry peers to share threat intelligence, best practices, and lessons learned from previous incidents, using forums such as ISACs or threat intelligence sharing platforms to exchange information, insights, and actionable intelligence on emerging threats, vulnerabilities, or attack trends, then using this collective knowledge to enhance the effectiveness and efficiency of threat hunting activities, enabling security teams to stay ahead of evolving threats and protect the organization from potential security risks or cyber threats. Incident response playbooks and procedures are fundamental components of an effective cybersecurity strategy, providing organizations with predefined workflows, guidelines, and best practices for responding to security incidents, breaches, or cyber threats in a structured and systematic manner, emphasizing a coordinated and proactive approach to incident detection, containment, eradication, and recovery, streamlining the response process and minimizing the impact of security incidents on the organization's operations, reputation, and bottom line. One essential aspect of incident response playbooks and procedures is the development of predefined incident response plans, which outline the roles, responsibilities, and actions to be taken by members of the incident response team during different phases of the incident response lifecycle, including preparation, detection, analysis, containment, eradication, recovery, and post-incident review, providing clear guidance and direction for responders to follow when responding to security incidents in a timely and effective manner, ensuring consistency, efficiency, and coordination in the response effort. Additionally, incident response playbooks often include predefined incident detection and alerting procedures, which outline the methods, tools, and techniques for monitoring, identifying, and prioritizing potential security incidents or anomalies within the organization's network environment, using tools such as SIEM (Security Information and Event Management) solutions or intrusion detection systems (IDS) to collect, correlate, and analyze security events and logs from various sources, then using predefined rules, signatures, or thresholds to generate alerts or notifications for suspicious activities, unauthorized access attempts, or abnormal behavior that may indicate the presence of a security incident or breach, enabling responders to promptly investigate and respond to potential threats before they escalate into significant security incidents or breaches. Furthermore, incident response playbooks often include predefined incident classification and triage procedures, which outline the criteria, severity levels, and impact assessments for categorizing and prioritizing security incidents based on their potential risk, impact, and urgency to the organization's operations, assets, or reputation, using predefined incident classification frameworks such as the Common Vulnerability Scoring System (CVSS) or the NIST Incident Response Guide to assign severity levels, priority levels, or response categories to different types of security incidents, then using predefined escalation paths, notification procedures, or response workflows to ensure that incidents are triaged, prioritized, and escalated to the appropriate stakeholders or response teams for further investigation and action, enabling responders to focus their efforts and resources on addressing the most critical and high-impact security incidents first, thereby minimizing the potential impact and consequences of security breaches on the organization's operations, assets, or reputation. Moreover, incident response playbooks often include predefined incident containment and eradication procedures, which outline the steps, methods, and techniques for isolating, mitigating, and remedying security incidents or breaches to prevent further damage, loss, or unauthorized access to the organization's systems, data, or resources, using tools such as firewalls, access controls, or endpoint security solutions to contain and quarantine affected systems or networks, then using predefined remediation and cleanup procedures, such as patching, malware removal, or data restoration, to eradicate malicious activity, remove unauthorized access, and restore affected systems to a secure and operational state, enabling responders to minimize the duration, scope, and impact of security incidents on the organization's operations, assets, or reputation, while also preventing the recurrence of similar incidents in the future. Additionally, incident response playbooks often include predefined incident communication and reporting procedures, which outline the channels, stakeholders, and messages to be used for communicating with internal and external parties during a security incident or breach, including employees, management, customers, partners, regulators, law enforcement, or the media, using predefined communication templates, scripts, or guidelines to ensure clear, timely, and consistent communication of incident-related information, updates, and instructions to all relevant parties, then using predefined reporting templates, formats, or protocols to document and report on the incident response activities, findings, and outcomes for internal review, regulatory compliance, or legal purposes, enabling responders to maintain transparency, accountability, and trust with stakeholders throughout the incident response process, while also meeting regulatory requirements and legal obligations related to incident reporting, disclosure, or notification. Furthermore, incident response playbooks often include predefined incident recovery and post-incident review procedures, which outline the steps, measures, and best practices for restoring affected systems, data, or services to a normal and secure state following a security incident or breach, using predefined recovery plans, backup procedures, or disaster recovery strategies to restore data from backups, rebuild compromised systems, or reconfigure affected services, then using predefined post-incident review processes, such as lessons learned sessions, root cause analyses, or incident retrospectives, to evaluate the effectiveness of the incident response effort, identify areas for improvement, and implement corrective actions or enhancements to the incident response playbook, procedures, or controls, enabling responders to learn from past incidents, strengthen their incident response capabilities, and better prepare for future security incidents or breaches, thereby enhancing the organization's overall resilience, readiness, and response to cyber threats and attacks.

BOOK 3
PENTEST+ EXAM PASS
NETWORK EXPLOITATION AND DEFENSE STRATEGIES

ROB BOTWRIGHT

Chapter 1: Network Enumeration and Scanning Techniques

Host discovery methods are essential techniques used in network reconnaissance to identify active hosts within a network environment, enabling security professionals to map the network topology, assess the scope of the network, and identify potential targets for further assessment or exploitation, emphasizing the importance of host discovery as a foundational step in the penetration testing process, allowing testers to gather critical information about the network infrastructure, including IP addresses, hostnames, and operating systems, which can be used to assess the security posture of the network and identify potential vulnerabilities or misconfigurations that may pose security risks, facilitating the identification of live hosts on a network is crucial for understanding the network's layout and potential attack surface, allowing security professionals to target specific systems for further analysis or exploitation, helping to prioritize security assessments and focus efforts on areas of the network that are most likely to contain valuable assets or sensitive information, leveraging various techniques and tools to perform host discovery, including ICMP (Internet Control

Message Protocol) ping sweeps, ARP (Address Resolution Protocol) scanning, and TCP (Transmission Control Protocol) SYN scans, each method has its advantages and limitations, and security professionals may choose to use one or more techniques depending on the specific requirements of the engagement and the network environment being assessed, ICMP ping sweeps are commonly used to determine the reachability of hosts on a network by sending ICMP echo requests to a range of IP addresses and waiting for responses, allowing testers to identify live hosts that respond to ping requests, however, ICMP ping sweeps may not detect hosts that have ICMP echo request/reply messages disabled or filtered by firewalls or intrusion prevention systems, limiting their effectiveness in certain network environments, ARP scanning is another host discovery technique that leverages the Address Resolution Protocol to map IP addresses to MAC (Media Access Control) addresses on a local network segment, enabling testers to identify live hosts by sending ARP requests and listening for responses, which can reveal the presence of active hosts on the local network segment, including devices such as routers, switches, and servers, however, ARP scanning is limited to the local network segment and may not be effective for discovering hosts across multiple network segments or subnets, TCP SYN scans, also known as TCP half-open scans, are a more stealthy host discovery technique that leverages the three-way TCP handshake to determine the reachability of hosts on a network, allowing testers to identify live hosts without completing the full TCP connection establishment process, which can help avoid detection by intrusion detection systems and firewall logs, making it a preferred technique for reconnaissance in adversarial environments, however, TCP SYN scans may be slower than ICMP ping sweeps or ARP scans and may not detect hosts that do not respond to TCP SYN packets or have TCP/IP stack implementations that deviate from the standard behavior, limiting their effectiveness in certain scenarios, in addition to these traditional host discovery methods, there are also more advanced techniques and tools available for identifying hosts on a network, including passive network monitoring, which involves capturing and analyzing network traffic to identify active hosts based on observed communication patterns, such as DNS (Domain Name System) queries, DHCP (Dynamic Host Configuration Protocol) requests, or network service announcements, without sending any packets directly to the hosts, making it a stealthy and non-intrusive method of host discovery, ideal for environments where active scanning may be prohibited or detected, however, passive network monitoring requires access to network traffic and may not be practical in all network environments, particularly those with encrypted or segmented traffic, limiting its applicability in certain scenarios, another advanced host discovery technique is network fingerprinting, which involves analyzing network responses to determine the type and version of operating systems and services running on hosts, allowing testers to identify potential targets for further analysis or exploitation based on known vulnerabilities or weaknesses associated with specific operating systems or applications, tools such as Nmap, Netdiscover, and Wireshark are commonly used for host discovery in penetration testing and cybersecurity assessments, providing security professionals with the ability to perform comprehensive host discovery using a variety of techniques and methodologies, enabling them to gather critical information about the network environment, assess its security posture, and identify potential risks or vulnerabilities that may pose security threats to the organization, ultimately, host discovery plays a crucial role in the reconnaissance phase of penetration testing and cybersecurity assessments, providing security professionals with the visibility and insight needed to understand the network infrastructure, identify potential targets, and prioritize security assessments, helping organizations strengthen their security defenses and mitigate the risks posed by cyber threats and attacks. Port scanning techniques are fundamental tools and methodologies used in network reconnaissance to identify open ports and services running on target systems, enabling security professionals to assess the security posture of a network, identify potential vulnerabilities, and prioritize security assessments, emphasizing the importance of port scanning as a critical step in the penetration testing process, allowing testers to gather valuable information about the network infrastructure, including the types of services and applications running on target systems, which can be used to assess the attack surface and identify potential entry points for exploitation, leveraging various port scanning techniques and tools to probe target systems and identify open ports, including TCP (Transmission Control Protocol) SYN scans, TCP connect scans, UDP (User Datagram Protocol) scans, and stealth scans, each technique has its advantages and limitations, and security professionals may choose to use one or more techniques depending on the specific requirements of the engagement and the network environment being assessed, TCP SYN scans, also known as half-open scans, are one of the most common and widely used port scanning techniques, which leverage the three-way TCP handshake to determine the state of TCP ports on target systems, allowing testers to identify open ports without establishing a full TCP connection, which can help avoid detection by intrusion detection systems and firewall logs, making it a preferred technique for reconnaissance in adversarial environments, the command to perform a TCP SYN scan using the Nmap tool is nmap -sS <target>, where <target> is the IP address or hostname of the target system, however, TCP SYN scans may be slower than other scanning techniques and may not detect ports that are protected by stateful firewalls or other network filtering devices, limiting their effectiveness in certain scenarios, TCP connect scans are another commonly used port scanning technique, which establish a full TCP connection with each port on the target system to determine its state, allowing testers to identify open ports by successfully establishing a connection, the command to perform a TCP connect scan using the Nmap tool is nmap -sT <target>, where <target> is the IP address or hostname of the target system, TCP connect scans are more reliable than TCP SYN scans and can detect ports that are protected by firewalls or other filtering devices, however, they are also more detectable and may generate more noise on the network, making them less stealthy than TCP SYN scans, UDP scans are used to identify open UDP ports on target systems, which are commonly used for services such as DNS, DHCP, and SNMP, the command to perform a UDP scan using the Nmap tool is nmap -sU <target>, where <target> is the IP address or hostname of the target system, UDP scans are slower and less reliable than TCP scans due to the connectionless nature of the UDP protocol, but they can help identify potential vulnerabilities or misconfigurations in UDP-based services, such as improperly configured firewalls or services running outdated software, stealth scans, such as TCP NULL scans, FIN scans, and Xmas scans, are designed to evade detection by intrusion detection systems and firewall logs by sending specially crafted packets that do not elicit a response from the target system, the command to perform a TCP NULL scan using the Nmap tool is nmap -sN <target>, where <target> is the IP address or hostname of the target system, stealth scans can be effective for reconnaissance in highly secure or monitored environments, but they may also be less reliable and may not detect all open ports on target systems, security professionals should carefully consider the advantages and limitations of each port scanning technique when planning and conducting network reconnaissance, taking into account factors such as network topology, target environment, and security requirements, to ensure thorough and accurate identification of open ports and services, enabling them to assess the security posture of the network and identify potential risks or vulnerabilities that may pose security threats to the organization, ultimately, port scanning plays a crucial role in the reconnaissance phase of penetration testing and cybersecurity assessments, providing security professionals with the visibility and insight needed to understand the network infrastructure, identify potential entry points for exploitation, and prioritize security assessments, helping organizations strengthen their security defenses and mitigate the risks posed by cyber threats and attacks.

Chapter 2: Exploiting Network Services

Exploiting common network services is a critical aspect of penetration testing and cybersecurity assessments, involving the identification and exploitation of vulnerabilities in widely used network services and protocols to gain unauthorized access to target systems or networks, emphasizing the importance of understanding common network services and their associated vulnerabilities as part of a comprehensive security testing strategy, enabling security professionals to assess the security posture of networked systems and identify potential risks or weaknesses that may pose security threats to the organization, leveraging various techniques and tools to identify and exploit vulnerabilities in common network services, including web servers, email servers, file transfer protocols, database servers, and network infrastructure devices, such as routers, switches, and firewalls, understanding the inherent risks associated with each network service and protocol, including known vulnerabilities, misconfigurations, and default settings that may expose systems to exploitation, is essential for effectively identifying and mitigating security risks, ensuring that network services are properly configured, patched, and hardened against potential attacks, minimizing the likelihood of successful exploitation and unauthorized access, the command to perform a vulnerability scan using the Nmap tool is nmap -p <port> --script <script> <target>, where <port> is the port number associated with the target service, <script> is the name of the Nmap script used to detect vulnerabilities in the service, and <target> is the IP address or hostname of the target system, for example, to scan for vulnerabilities in an HTTP web server running on port 80, the command would be nmap -p 80 --script http-vuln-cve2017-5638 <target>, understanding the common vulnerabilities and attack vectors associated with web servers, such as SQL injection, cross-site scripting (XSS), and remote code execution (RCE), is essential for identifying and exploiting security weaknesses in web applications and services, enabling attackers to compromise systems, steal sensitive data, or launch further attacks against other systems or users, for example, to exploit an SQL injection vulnerability in a web application, an attacker could use tools such as SQLMap or Burp Suite to craft malicious SQL queries and inject them into input fields or parameters, exploiting vulnerabilities in email servers and protocols, such as SMTP (Simple Mail Transfer Protocol) and IMAP (Internet Message Access Protocol), can enable attackers to bypass email filtering mechanisms, spoof email addresses, or execute arbitrary code on target systems, allowing them to launch phishing attacks, distribute malware, or steal sensitive information, for example, to exploit an SMTP server using a command injection vulnerability, an attacker could use the telnet command to connect to the SMTP server and inject malicious commands into email headers or message bodies, exploiting vulnerabilities in file transfer protocols, such as FTP (File Transfer Protocol) and SMB (Server Message Block), can enable attackers to gain unauthorized access to files and directories on target systems, allowing them to exfiltrate sensitive data, upload malicious files, or execute arbitrary commands, for example, to exploit an SMB server using a known vulnerability, an attacker could use the Metasploit framework to exploit the EternalBlue vulnerability (CVE-2017-0144) and gain remote code execution on a target system, exploiting vulnerabilities in database servers, such as MySQL, PostgreSQL, and Microsoft SQL Server, can enable attackers to access or manipulate sensitive data stored in databases, exfiltrate database contents, or execute arbitrary SQL queries, for example, to exploit a SQL injection vulnerability in a MySQL database, an attacker could use tools such as SQLMap or Burp Suite to inject malicious SQL queries into input fields or parameters and retrieve sensitive information from the database, exploiting vulnerabilities in network infrastructure devices, such as routers, switches, and firewalls, can enable attackers to gain unauthorized access to network resources, intercept or modify network traffic, or disrupt network operations, for example, to exploit a remote code execution vulnerability in a Cisco router, an attacker could use the Metasploit framework to exploit the vulnerability and gain privileged access to the router, ultimately, understanding and exploiting common network services is a critical skill for security professionals involved in penetration testing, red teaming, and cybersecurity assessments, enabling them to identify and mitigate security risks, strengthen defenses, and protect against cyber threats and attacks.

Chapter 3: Firewall Evasion Techniques

Firewall identification and enumeration are essential steps in assessing the security posture of a network, involving the identification and analysis of firewall devices deployed to protect network assets and control the flow of traffic between different network segments, emphasizing the importance of understanding firewall configurations, rulesets, and filtering policies to identify potential security weaknesses or misconfigurations that may expose systems to exploitation or unauthorized access, leveraging various techniques and tools to identify and enumerate firewall devices and their associated configurations, including network scanning, banner grabbing, port scanning, and protocol analysis, understanding the different types of firewalls commonly used in network environments, including stateful firewalls, stateless firewalls, application-layer firewalls, and next-generation firewalls, each with its unique capabilities, features, and limitations, enabling security professionals to accurately identify and assess firewall devices deployed within the network, the command to perform a basic network scan using the Nmap tool is nmap -sP <target>, where <target> is the IP address range or subnet to be scanned, allowing testers to identify live hosts and devices on the network, for example, to scan the entire 192.168.1.0/24 subnet, the command would be nmap -sP 192.168.1.0/24, the command to perform banner grabbing and service enumeration using the Nmap tool is nmap -sV <target>, where <target> is the IP address or hostname of the target system, enabling testers to identify the types and versions of services running on open ports, for example, to perform service enumeration on a target system with the IP address 192.168.1.100, the command would be nmap -sV 192.168.1.100, port scanning techniques, such as TCP SYN scans, TCP connect scans, and UDP scans, can be used to identify open ports and services on target systems, allowing testers to identify potential entry points for exploitation and assess the effectiveness of firewall filtering policies, understanding firewall logging and monitoring capabilities, including the types of events and data collected by firewalls, such as connection logs, packet logs, and security alerts, enabling security professionals to identify and analyze firewall events and activities for potential security incidents or anomalies, leveraging protocol analysis techniques, such as packet sniffing and traffic analysis, to identify and analyze network traffic passing through firewall devices, enabling testers to understand how traffic is filtered, routed, and controlled by firewalls and identify potential security weaknesses or misconfigurations, understanding common misconfigurations and vulnerabilities associated with firewall devices, such as default credentials, weak encryption algorithms, and improper rule configurations, enabling security professionals to identify and remediate security weaknesses or vulnerabilities that may expose systems to exploitation or unauthorized access, ultimately, firewall identification and enumeration play a crucial role in assessing the security posture of a network, enabling security professionals to identify, analyze, and mitigate potential security risks or vulnerabilities associated with firewall devices, strengthen network defenses, and protect against cyber threats and attacks. Firewall rule bypass methods are crucial techniques employed in cybersecurity assessments to circumvent or evade firewall filtering policies and access restricted resources or services within a network, highlighting the significance of understanding various tactics and strategies used to bypass firewall rules to identify potential vulnerabilities and weaknesses in network defenses, leveraging a combination of reconnaissance, exploitation, and evasion techniques to bypass firewall rules, including application-layer protocols, covert channels, tunneling protocols, and protocol smuggling, enabling attackers to bypass firewall restrictions and establish unauthorized connections or access resources within the network, the command to perform a port scan using the Nmap tool is nmap -p <port> <target>, where <port> is the specific port number to be scanned, and <target> is the IP address or hostname of the target system, allowing testers to identify open ports and services that may be accessible despite firewall restrictions, for example, to scan for open ports on a target system with the IP address 192.168.1.100, the command would be nmap -p 1-65535 192.168.1.100, application-layer protocols, such as HTTP, HTTPS, and DNS, can be leveraged to bypass firewall rules by disguising malicious traffic as legitimate application data, enabling attackers to evade detection and bypass filtering policies by using common application-layer protocols and ports, covert channels, such as steganography, covert timing channels, and data obfuscation techniques, can be used to hide malicious traffic within seemingly innocuous communication channels or data streams, enabling attackers to bypass firewall restrictions and exfiltrate sensitive information without detection, tunneling protocols, such as SSH tunneling, VPN tunneling, and ICMP tunneling, can be used to bypass firewall restrictions by encapsulating malicious traffic within legitimate network protocols or encrypted communication channels, enabling attackers to establish covert communication channels or access restricted resources within the network, protocol smuggling techniques, such as HTTP request smuggling, TCP/IP fragmentation, and IP address spoofing, can be used to exploit inconsistencies or vulnerabilities in firewall implementations and inspection mechanisms, enabling attackers to bypass firewall restrictions and execute arbitrary commands or access sensitive information within the network, understanding the limitations and vulnerabilities associated with firewall devices, such as stateful packet inspection, deep packet inspection, and application-layer filtering, is essential for identifying potential weaknesses or bypass techniques that may be exploited by attackers to bypass firewall rules and compromise network security, leveraging evasion techniques, such as packet fragmentation, traffic fragmentation, and traffic obfuscation, can be used to evade firewall detection mechanisms and disguise malicious traffic as legitimate network data, enabling attackers to bypass firewall rules and access restricted resources or services within the network, ultimately, understanding firewall rule bypass methods is crucial for security professionals involved in penetration testing, red teaming, and cybersecurity assessments, enabling them to identify and mitigate potential vulnerabilities or weaknesses in firewall configurations, strengthen network defenses, and protect against advanced cyber threats and attacks.

Chapter 4: Intrusion Detection and Prevention Systems

Evading IDS/IPS detection is a critical aspect of penetration testing and cybersecurity assessments, involving the circumvention or evasion of intrusion detection systems (IDS) and intrusion prevention systems (IPS) to avoid detection and execute malicious activities within a network, highlighting the importance of understanding various evasion techniques and strategies used by attackers to bypass IDS/IPS defenses and evade detection, leveraging a combination of stealth, obfuscation, and evasion techniques to evade detection by IDS/IPS devices, including packet fragmentation, traffic encryption, protocol evasion, and signature evasion, enabling attackers to bypass detection mechanisms and carry out unauthorized activities without triggering alerts or alarms, the command to perform a packet capture using the Wireshark tool is wireshark -i <interface>, where <interface> is the network interface on which to capture packets, allowing testers to capture and analyze network traffic for potential evasion techniques or suspicious activities, for example, to capture packets on the eth0 network interface, the command would be wireshark -i eth0, packet fragmentation techniques, such as IP fragmentation and TCP segmentation, can be used to evade IDS/IPS detection by breaking large packets into smaller fragments that are less likely to be detected or inspected by intrusion detection systems, enabling attackers to evade detection mechanisms and avoid triggering alerts or alarms, traffic encryption techniques, such as SSL/TLS encryption, VPN tunneling, and SSH tunneling, can be used to encrypt malicious traffic and disguise it as legitimate communication, enabling attackers to evade detection by IDS/IPS devices and carry out unauthorized activities without detection, protocol evasion techniques, such as protocol tunneling, protocol normalization, and protocol spoofing, can be used to bypass IDS/IPS detection by disguising malicious traffic as legitimate network protocols or by exploiting vulnerabilities in protocol implementations, enabling attackers to evade detection mechanisms and avoid triggering alerts or alarms, signature evasion techniques, such as polymorphic malware, obfuscated code, and zero-day exploits, can be used to bypass IDS/IPS detection by modifying or encrypting malicious code to evade signature-based detection mechanisms, enabling attackers to evade detection and carry out stealthy attacks without detection, understanding the limitations and vulnerabilities associated with IDS/IPS devices, such as signature-based detection, anomaly-based detection, and heuristic analysis, is essential for identifying potential weaknesses or evasion techniques that may be exploited by attackers to bypass IDS/IPS defenses and compromise network security, leveraging evasion techniques, such as traffic shaping, traffic splitting, and traffic redirection, can be used to evade detection by IDS/IPS devices and disguise malicious traffic as legitimate network data, enabling attackers to carry out stealthy attacks and avoid detection, ultimately, evading IDS/IPS detection is a critical skill for security professionals involved in penetration testing, red teaming, and cybersecurity assessments, enabling them to identify and mitigate potential vulnerabilities or weaknesses in IDS/IPS configurations, strengthen network defenses, and protect against advanced cyber threats and attacks. Detecting and responding to intrusions are fundamental components of cybersecurity operations, involving the identification, analysis, and mitigation of unauthorized activities or security breaches within a network or system, highlighting the significance of implementing effective intrusion detection and response (IDR) strategies to detect, investigate, and mitigate security incidents in a timely manner, the command to check the system logs for suspicious activities using the Linux journalctl command is journalctl -xe, enabling system administrators to review system logs and identify potential indicators of compromise (IOCs) or suspicious behavior that may indicate a security breach, for example, to display all recent log entries, the command would be journalctl -xe, intrusion detection systems (IDS), intrusion prevention systems (IPS), and security information and event management (SIEM) solutions are commonly used to detect and alert on suspicious activities or anomalies within a network or system, leveraging a combination of signature-based detection, anomaly detection, and behavioral analysis techniques to identify potential security incidents, the command to monitor network traffic using the tcpdump tool is tcpdump -i <interface>, where <interface> is the network interface on which to capture packets, allowing network administrators to capture and analyze network traffic for potential signs of malicious activity or intrusion attempts, for example, to capture packets on the eth0 network interface, the command would be tcpdump -i eth0, endpoint detection and response

(EDR) solutions are used to monitor and protect endpoints, such as desktops, laptops, and servers, against advanced threats and malware, enabling organizations to detect, investigate, and respond to security incidents at the endpoint level, the command to scan a system for malware using the Windows Defender command-line utility is MpCmdRun.exe -Scan -ScanType 3, enabling system administrators to initiate a malware scan and detect potential threats on a Windows system, for example, to perform a full system scan, the command would be MpCmdRun.exe -Scan -ScanType 3, security information and event management (SIEM) solutions aggregate, correlate, and analyze log data from various sources, such as network devices, servers, and applications, to provide real-time visibility into security events and incidents, enabling organizations to detect and respond to intrusions more effectively, the command to search for a specific event in the Windows event logs using the Get-WinEvent PowerShell cmdlet is Get-WinEvent -LogName <logname> -FilterXPath "<query>", where <logname> is the name of the event log to search, and <query> is the XPath query used to filter events, allowing system administrators to search for specific events or log entries related to security incidents, for example, to search for failed login attempts in the Security event log, the command would be Get-WinEvent -LogName Security -FilterXPath "EventID=4625", incident response teams follow predefined procedures and playbooks to respond to security incidents in a structured and coordinated manner, involving steps such as incident triage, containment, eradication, recovery, and lessons learned, enabling organizations to minimize the impact of security breaches and prevent future incidents, ultimately, detecting and responding to intrusions is a critical aspect of cybersecurity operations, enabling organizations to protect their assets, data, and reputation from cyber threats and attacks.

Chapter 5: Active Directory Enumeration and Exploitation

Enumerating Active Directory objects is a crucial step in penetration testing and cybersecurity assessments, involving the systematic discovery and enumeration of users, groups, computers, and other objects within an Active Directory domain, highlighting the importance of understanding various enumeration techniques and tools used to gather information about the network infrastructure and identify potential security vulnerabilities or misconfigurations, the command to enumerate Active Directory objects using the LDAP protocol is ldapsearch, enabling testers to query the Active Directory Lightweight Directory Services (AD LDS) or other LDAP-compatible directory services for information about directory objects, such as users, groups, and organizational units, for example, to search for all users in the domain, the command would be ldapsearch -x -h <domain_controller_ip> -b "dc=<domain>,dc=<com>" "(objectClass=user)", where <domain_controller_ip> is the IP address of the domain controller and <domain> is the name of the Active Directory domain, enumeration techniques include querying domain controllers, performing network reconnaissance, and analyzing Active Directory configuration information, enabling testers to gather information about the domain structure, user accounts, group memberships, and computer resources, the command to query domain controllers for domain information using the nltest tool is nltest /dclist:<domain>, allowing testers to enumerate domain controllers and gather information about the domain, such as the domain name, domain controller names, and site information, for example, to list the domain controllers for the contoso.com domain, the command would be nltest /dclist:contoso.com, network reconnaissance techniques, such as DNS enumeration, port scanning, and service enumeration, can be used to gather information about the Active Directory environment, including domain names, IP addresses, hostnames, and network services, enabling testers to identify potential targets and attack vectors, the command to perform DNS enumeration using the nslookup tool is nslookup -type=srv _ldap._tcp.<domain>, allowing testers to enumerate LDAP service records in DNS and gather information about domain controllers, for example, to enumerate LDAP service records for the contoso.com domain, the command would be nslookup -type=srv _ldap._tcp.contoso.com, analyzing Active Directory configuration information, such as group policy settings, domain trust relationships, and service principal names (SPNs), can provide valuable insights into the security posture and attack surface of the domain, enabling testers to identify potential weaknesses or misconfigurations that may be exploited during penetration testing, the command to list group policy objects (GPOs) using the PowerShell Get-GPO cmdlet is Get-GPO -All, allowing testers to enumerate all group policy objects in the domain and gather information about their settings and configurations, for example, to list all GPOs in the domain, the command would be Get-GPO -All, ultimately, enumerating Active Directory objects is a critical aspect of penetration testing and security assessments, enabling testers to gather information about the domain environment and identify potential security risks or weaknesses that may be exploited by attackers. Exploiting Active Directory misconfigurations is a common tactic used by attackers to gain unauthorized access to an organization's network resources and sensitive data, underscoring the importance of identifying and remedying misconfigurations to enhance the overall security posture of the Active Directory environment, the command to enumerate Active Directory domain controllers using the nltest utility in Windows Command Prompt is nltest /dclist:<domain>, enabling testers to gather information about domain controllers and their associated domains, for instance, to list domain controllers for the contoso.com domain, the command would be nltest /dclist:contoso.com, misconfigurations in Active Directory can arise from various sources, including improper access control settings, weak authentication mechanisms, and inadequate security configurations, which can leave the network vulnerable to exploitation and compromise, the command to list all users in an Active Directory domain using the net user command in Command Prompt is net user /domain, allowing testers to enumerate all user accounts in the domain, for example, to list all users in the contoso.com domain, the command would be net user /domain, common misconfigurations in Active Directory include weak or default passwords, excessive user privileges, insecure group memberships, and misconfigured access control lists (ACLs), which can provide attackers with opportunities to escalate privileges, execute arbitrary code, and gain unauthorized access to critical systems and data, the command to list all group policy objects (GPOs) in an Active Directory domain using the PowerShell Get-GPO cmdlet is Get-GPO -All, enabling testers to enumerate all GPOs and analyze their configurations for potential misconfigurations or vulnerabilities, for instance, to list all GPOs in the domain, the command would be Get-GPO -All, improper delegation of administrative privileges, misconfigured group memberships, and insecure service configurations are common misconfigurations that can lead to unauthorized access and compromise of Active Directory resources, the command to check the permissions on a specific Active Directory object using the dsacls command in Command Prompt is dsacls <distinguished_name>, allowing testers to view the access control list (ACL) for the specified object, such as a user account or organizational unit (OU), for example, to view the permissions for the Marketing OU, the command would be dsacls "OU=Marketing,DC=contoso,DC=com", leveraging misconfigured trust relationships, unsecure LDAP configurations, and weak authentication protocols, attackers can exploit Active Directory misconfigurations to move laterally within the network, escalate privileges, and exfiltrate sensitive data, the command to identify insecure LDAP configurations using the ldapsearch utility in Linux Command Line is ldapsearch -x -H ldap://<domain_controller_ip> -b "" -s base -LLL supportedSASLMechanisms, enabling testers to enumerate supported LDAP authentication mechanisms on the domain controller, for instance, to query the domain controller with the IP address 192.168.1.100, the command would be ldapsearch -x -H ldap://192.168.1.100 -b "" -s base -LLL supportedSASLMechanisms, overall, exploiting Active Directory misconfigurations requires a deep understanding of the Active Directory environment, security principles, and common attack techniques, enabling testers to identify, exploit, and remediate misconfigurations to improve the overall security posture of the network.

Chapter 6: Wireless Network Exploitation and Defense

Wireless attack surface analysis is a critical aspect of cybersecurity assessments, focusing on identifying and evaluating vulnerabilities and potential attack vectors within wireless networks to enhance overall security posture and mitigate risks, the command to perform a wireless site survey using the airodump-ng tool in Kali Linux is airodump-ng <interface>, allowing testers to capture and analyze wireless network traffic, for example, to perform a site survey on the wireless interface wlan0, the command would be airodump-ng wlan0, wireless networks present unique security challenges due to their inherent vulnerabilities, such as weak encryption, unauthorized access points, and rogue devices, which can be exploited by attackers to gain unauthorized access to network resources and sensitive information, the command to scan for nearby wireless networks using the iwlist utility in Linux Terminal is iwlist <interface> scan, enabling testers to enumerate nearby wireless access points and gather information about their configurations, for instance, to scan for nearby networks on the wireless interface wlan0, the command would be iwlist wlan0 scan, conducting a thorough wireless attack surface analysis involves several key steps, including identifying wireless access points, assessing signal strength and coverage areas, analyzing encryption methods and security protocols, and detecting rogue devices, the command to display detailed information about a specific wireless network using the iw utility in Linux Terminal is iw <interface> info, allowing testers to view information about the configured wireless interface and associated networks, for example, to display information about the wireless interface wlan0, the command would be iw wlan0 info, identifying wireless access points and associated clients is a fundamental step in wireless attack surface analysis, enabling testers to enumerate available networks, assess signal strength, and identify potential targets for exploitation, the command to list nearby wireless access points using the iw dev command in Linux Terminal is iw dev <interface> scan | grep "SSID", allowing testers to filter scan results for the SSID (Service Set Identifier) of nearby networks, for instance, to list nearby access points on the wireless interface wlan0, the command would be iw dev wlan0 scan | grep "SSID", assessing signal strength and coverage areas is essential for determining the reach and effectiveness of wireless networks, enabling testers to identify potential blind spots and areas of weak signal coverage that may be susceptible to unauthorized access, the command to display signal strength and signal quality for nearby wireless networks using the iwlist utility in Linux Terminal is iwlist <interface> scan | grep "Signal", for example, to display signal strength for nearby networks on the wireless interface wlan0, the command would be iwlist wlan0 scan | grep "Signal", analyzing encryption methods and security protocols is crucial for evaluating the security posture of wireless networks, enabling testers to identify weak encryption methods, outdated security protocols, and potential vulnerabilities that may be exploited by attackers, the command to display encryption and authentication information for a specific wireless network using the iwconfig utility in Linux Terminal is iwconfig <interface>, allowing testers to view encryption and authentication settings for the configured wireless interface, for instance, to display encryption information for the wireless interface wlan0, the command would be iwconfig wlan0, detecting rogue devices and unauthorized access points is critical for preventing unauthorized access and maintaining the integrity of wireless networks, enabling testers to identify and mitigate potential security threats and vulnerabilities, the command to scan for nearby wireless devices using the airmon-ng tool in Kali Linux is airmon-ng start <interface>, followed by airodump-ng mon0, allowing testers to put the wireless interface into monitor mode and scan for nearby devices, for example, to start monitor mode on the wireless interface wlan0 and scan for nearby devices, the commands would be airmon-ng start wlan0 and airodump-ng mon0, overall, conducting a comprehensive wireless attack surface analysis is essential for identifying vulnerabilities, assessing risks, and implementing effective security measures to protect wireless networks from unauthorized access and exploitation.

Wireless security best practices are essential for safeguarding wireless networks against unauthorized access, data breaches, and cyber attacks, the command to configure a strong Wi-Fi password using the wpa_passphrase utility in Linux Terminal is wpa_passphrase <SSID> <password>, enabling administrators to generate a hashed passphrase for securing Wi-Fi networks, for instance, to generate a hashed passphrase for the SSID "example_network" with the password "securepassword123", the command would be wpa_passphrase example_network securepassword123, implementing strong encryption protocols, such as WPA2 (Wi-Fi Protected Access 2) or WPA3, is crucial for protecting wireless networks from eavesdropping and unauthorized access, the command to configure a wireless network interface with WPA2 encryption using the wpa_supplicant.conf file in Linux Terminal is wpa_passphrase <SSID> <password> >> /etc/wpa_supplicant/wpa_supplicant.conf, followed by wpa_supplicant -B -i <interface> -c /etc/wpa_supplicant/wpa_supplicant.conf, enabling administrators to securely connect to a Wi-Fi network using WPA2 encryption, for example, to configure a wireless interface "wlan0" with WPA2 encryption for the SSID "example_network" and password "securepassword123", the commands would be wpa_passphrase example_network securepassword123 >> /etc/wpa_supplicant/wpa_supplicant.conf and wpa_supplicant -B -i wlan0 -c /etc/wpa_supplicant/wpa_supplicant.conf,

disabling SSID broadcasting can help prevent unauthorized users from discovering and connecting to wireless networks, the command to disable SSID broadcasting on a wireless access point using the iwconfig utility in Linux Terminal is iwconfig <interface> essid off, for instance, to disable SSID broadcasting on the wireless interface "wlan0", the command would be iwconfig wlan0 essid off, enabling MAC address filtering can restrict access to wireless networks based on the MAC (Media Access Control) addresses of devices, the command to add a MAC address to the allowed list on a wireless router using the router's web interface is to log in to the router's administration panel, navigate to the MAC address filtering settings, and add the MAC address of the device to the allowed list, implementing a firewall and intrusion detection system (IDS) on wireless networks can help detect and block suspicious network traffic and unauthorized access attempts, the command to configure a firewall rule to block incoming traffic from a specific IP address using the iptables utility in Linux Terminal is iptables -A INPUT -s <IP_address> -j DROP, enabling administrators to block incoming traffic from a specific IP address, for example, to block traffic from the IP address "192.168.1.100", the command would be iptables -A INPUT -s 192.168.1.100 -j DROP, regularly updating firmware and security patches on wireless routers and access points is essential for addressing known vulnerabilities and protecting against emerging threats, the command to check for available updates for a wireless router using the router's web interface is to log in to the router's administration panel, navigate to the firmware update section, and check for available updates, implementing strong authentication mechanisms, such as WPA2-Enterprise or 802.1X, can enhance the security of wireless networks by requiring users to authenticate with a username and password or digital certificate before connecting, the command to configure a wireless network interface with

WPA2-Enterprise authentication using the wpa_supplicant.conf file in Linux Terminal is wpa_supplicant -B -i <interface> -c /etc/wpa_supplicant/wpa_supplicant.conf, enabling administrators to configure a wireless interface for WPA2-Enterprise authentication, for example, to configure a wireless interface "wlan0" for WPA2-Enterprise authentication, the command would be wpa_supplicant -B -i wlan0 -c /etc/wpa_supplicant/wpa_supplicant.conf,

disabling Wi-Fi Protected Setup (WPS) can prevent brute-force attacks and unauthorized access to wireless networks, the command to disable WPS on a wireless router using the router's web interface is to log in to the router's administration panel, navigate to the WPS settings, and disable the WPS feature, educating users about the importance of wireless security and best practices, such as avoiding public Wi-Fi networks and using VPNs (Virtual Private Networks) when connecting to untrusted networks, can help mitigate the risk of security incidents and data breaches, the command to configure a wireless access point with a guest network using the router's web interface is to log in to the router's administration panel, navigate to the guest network settings, and configure the guest network with limited access privileges, such as restricted bandwidth and internet-only access, implementing physical security measures, such as placing wireless routers and access points in secure locations and using tamper-evident seals, can help prevent unauthorized access and tampering with network equipment, the command to configure a wireless network interface with a static IP address using the ifconfig utility in Linux Terminal is ifconfig <interface> <IP_address> netmask <subnet_mask>, enabling administrators to assign a static IP address to a wireless interface, for example, to assign the IP address "192.168.1.10" with a subnet mask of "255.255.255.0" to the wireless interface "wlan0", the command would be ifconfig wlan0 192.168.1.10 netmask 255.255.255.0, overall, implementing these wireless security best practices is crucial for protecting wireless networks from security threats and ensuring the confidentiality, integrity, and availability of sensitive information and resources.

Chapter 7: Cloud Infrastructure Security

Cloud computing has revolutionized the way businesses and individuals access, store, and manage data and applications, the command to deploy a virtual machine instance on a cloud platform like Amazon Web Services (AWS) using the AWS Management Console is to log in to the AWS Management Console, navigate to the EC2 (Elastic Compute Cloud) dashboard, and click on the "Launch Instance" button, enabling users to quickly provision computing resources on-demand without the need for physical hardware, for instance, to launch a new virtual machine instance, users can select an Amazon Machine Image (AMI), choose instance type, configure instance details, and add storage, security groups, and tags, the command to deploy a virtual machine instance on a cloud platform like Microsoft Azure using the Azure Portal is to log in to the Azure Portal, navigate to the Virtual Machines section, and click on the "Add" button, allowing users to create and manage virtual machines in the cloud, for example, to create a new virtual machine, users can select a base image, choose instance size, configure networking, and set up storage and monitoring options, cloud service models, including Infrastructure as a Service (IaaS),

Platform as a Service (PaaS), and Software as a Service (SaaS), offer different levels of abstraction and management responsibilities, the command to deploy a cloud-based application on a Platform as a Service (PaaS) provider like Heroku using the Heroku Command Line Interface (CLI) is heroku create, followed by git push heroku master, allowing developers to deploy applications without worrying about underlying infrastructure, for example, to deploy a Node.js application on Heroku, developers can create a new Heroku app using the heroku create command and then push the application code to the Heroku remote repository using git push heroku master, Infrastructure as a Service (IaaS) provides virtualized computing resources, such as virtual machines, storage, and networking, allowing users to deploy and manage their own operating systems, middleware, and applications, the command to deploy a virtual machine instance on a cloud platform like Google Cloud Platform (GCP) using the Google Cloud Console is to log in to the Google Cloud Console, navigate to the Compute Engine section, and click on the "Create Instance" button, enabling users to create and configure virtual machine instances in the cloud, for instance, to create a new virtual machine, users can choose a machine type, configure boot disk and networking options, and add metadata tags, Platform as a Service (PaaS) abstracts away the underlying infrastructure and provides a platform for developers to build, deploy, and manage applications, the command to deploy a cloud-based database on a Platform as a Service (PaaS) provider like MongoDB Atlas using the MongoDB Atlas web interface is to log in to the MongoDB Atlas web interface, navigate to the Clusters section, and click on the "Create Cluster" button, allowing users to deploy and manage MongoDB databases in the cloud, for example, to create a new MongoDB cluster, users can select a cloud provider, region, and cluster configuration options, Software as a Service (SaaS) delivers applications over the internet on a subscription basis, allowing users to access and use software without needing to install or manage it locally, the command to deploy a cloud-based email service on a Software as a Service (SaaS) provider like Microsoft Office 365 is to log in to the Microsoft 365 Admin Center, navigate to the Exchange section, and click on the "Add Users" button, enabling administrators to provision and manage email accounts for users in the cloud, for instance, to add a new user, administrators can enter user details, assign licenses, and configure mailbox settings, security considerations in cloud computing include data protection, identity and access management, network security, and compliance, the command to configure access control policies for cloud resources on a Platform as a Service (PaaS) provider like AWS using AWS Identity and Access Management (IAM) is to log in to the AWS Management Console, navigate to the IAM dashboard, and click on the "Policies" tab, allowing administrators to create and manage access control policies for users and groups, for example, to create a new IAM policy, administrators can define policy permissions using JSON syntax and attach the policy to IAM users or groups, implementing encryption for data at rest and in transit is essential for protecting sensitive information stored and transmitted in the cloud, the command to enable server-side encryption for data stored in an Amazon S3 bucket using the AWS Management Console is to log in to the AWS Management Console, navigate to the S3 dashboard, select the desired bucket, and click on the "Properties" tab, enabling administrators to configure server-side encryption using AWS Key Management Service (KMS) or AWS-managed keys, for instance, to enable server-side encryption with AWS-managed keys, administrators can select the "AES-256" encryption option and save the settings. Securing cloud infrastructure is paramount in today's digital landscape, where organizations rely heavily on cloud services to store, process, and manage their data and applications, the command to enable multi-factor authentication (MFA) for AWS user accounts using the AWS Management

Console is to log in to the AWS Management Console, navigate to the IAM dashboard, select the desired user, and click on the "Security credentials" tab, enabling administrators to configure MFA using a virtual or hardware MFA device, for example, to enable MFA for a user, administrators can choose the "Assign MFA device" option and follow the prompts to set up MFA, leveraging Identity and Access Management (IAM) is essential for controlling access to AWS resources and ensuring that only authorized users and applications can interact with them, the command to create an IAM role for accessing AWS services from an EC2 instance using the AWS Command Line Interface (CLI) is aws iam create-role, followed by aws iam attach-role-policy, enabling users to create IAM roles and attach policies to grant permissions to EC2 instances, for instance, to create an IAM role, users can specify the role name and trust policy using the --role-name and --assume-role-policy-document parameters, respectively, and then attach policies using the aws iam attach-role-policy command, implementing network security controls, such as Virtual Private Cloud (VPC) security groups and network access control lists (ACLs), is crucial for protecting cloud resources from unauthorized access and malicious attacks, the command to create a new security group for an EC2 instance using the AWS CLI is aws ec2 create-security-group, followed by aws ec2 authorize-security-group-ingress, enabling users to create security groups and define inbound and outbound traffic rules, for example, to create a security group, users can specify the group name and description using the --group-name and --description parameters, respectively, and then authorize inbound traffic using the aws ec2 authorize-security-group-ingress command, encrypting data at rest and in transit helps prevent unauthorized access to sensitive information stored in the cloud, the command to enable encryption for an Amazon RDS database instance using the AWS Management Console is to log in to the AWS Management Console, navigate to the RDS dashboard, select the desired database instance, and click on the "Modify" button, allowing administrators to enable encryption using AWS Key Management Service (KMS), for instance, to enable encryption, administrators can choose the desired encryption type (e.g., AWS managed keys or customer managed keys) and save the settings, regularly monitoring cloud infrastructure for security threats and vulnerabilities is essential for detecting and mitigating potential risks, the command to enable AWS CloudTrail logging for monitoring API activity using the AWS CLI is aws cloudtrail create-trail, followed by aws cloudtrail start-logging, enabling users to create and start logging API activity for AWS services, for example, to create a CloudTrail trail, users can specify the trail name, S3 bucket for log storage, and optional settings using the --name, --s3-bucket-name, and other parameters, respectively, and then start logging using the aws cloudtrail start-logging command.

Chapter 8: Buffer Overflow Attacks and Protections

Understanding buffer overflows is crucial in the realm of cybersecurity, as they remain one of the most common and dangerous vulnerabilities exploited by attackers, the command to compile a simple C program vulnerable to a buffer overflow using the GNU Compiler Collection (GCC) is gcc -o vulnerable_program vulnerable_program.c, illustrating how even seemingly innocuous code can become a gateway for malicious actors, buffer overflows occur when a program writes more data to a buffer than it can hold, causing the excess data to overwrite adjacent memory locations, this can lead to unintended consequences such as altering program behavior, crashing the program, or even allowing an attacker to execute arbitrary code, understanding the anatomy of a buffer overflow involves grasping concepts such as stack memory layout, function calls, return addresses, and the role of the stack pointer, for instance, the strcpy() function in C is notorious for its lack of bounds checking, making it vulnerable to buffer overflow attacks, an attacker can exploit this vulnerability by crafting a payload that exceeds the buffer's size, causing it to overwrite adjacent memory, including the return address, thus hijacking the program's control flow, mitigating buffer overflows requires a multifaceted approach encompassing secure coding practices, compiler-level protections, and runtime defenses, one such defense mechanism is stack canaries, which are random values placed between the buffer and the return address to detect buffer overflow attempts, the command to compile a C program with stack canaries enabled using GCC is gcc -o program program.c -fstack-protector, illustrating how compilers can insert additional security checks to thwart buffer overflow exploits, another mitigation technique is address space layout randomization (ASLR), which randomizes the memory addresses of executable code and data, making it harder for attackers to predict the location of vulnerable functions and variables, incorporating ASLR into the compilation process can be achieved with the -fPIE (Position Independent Executable) flag in GCC, for instance, gcc -o program program.c -fPIE -pie, demonstrating how ASLR adds an extra layer of protection against buffer overflow attacks, furthermore, modern programming languages such as Rust and Go are designed with memory safety features that mitigate common vulnerabilities like buffer overflows, making them less prone to such exploits, understanding the history of buffer overflows reveals their longstanding presence in computer security, with notable examples like the Morris Worm in 1988 exploiting vulnerabilities in the fingerd and sendmail utilities, today, buffer overflow vulnerabilities remain prevalent in software applications ranging from web servers to embedded systems, underscoring the importance of continued vigilance and proactive measures to address this persistent threat, conducting thorough code reviews and vulnerability assessments can help identify and remediate buffer overflow vulnerabilities early in the development lifecycle, the command to perform a static code analysis of a C program using a tool like cppcheck is cppcheck program.c, enabling developers to detect potential buffer overflow issues and other coding errors before they manifest in deployed software, In summary, understanding buffer overflows is essential for both developers and cybersecurity professionals to protect against one of the most insidious and widespread threats in the digital landscape. Buffer overflow protection mechanisms are vital components in modern cybersecurity strategies, as they help mitigate one of the most common and severe vulnerabilities in software systems, one such mechanism is stack canaries, which act as guard values placed between the buffer and the return address on the stack to detect buffer overflow attempts, the command to compile a C program with stack canaries enabled using the GNU Compiler Collection (GCC) is gcc -o program

program.c -fstack-protector, demonstrating how compilers can automatically insert these security checks into the generated executable, another important protection mechanism is address space layout randomization (ASLR), which randomizes the memory addresses of executable code and data segments, making it harder for attackers to predict the location of vulnerable functions and variables, incorporating ASLR into the compilation process can be achieved with the -fPIE (Position Independent Executable) flag in GCC, for instance, gcc -o program program.c -fPIE -pie, showcasing how ASLR adds an extra layer of defense against buffer overflow exploits, data execution prevention (DEP) is another key defense mechanism that helps prevent buffer overflow attacks by marking certain memory regions as non-executable, thus preventing attackers from injecting and executing malicious code in these areas, enabling DEP on Windows systems can be done through the Data Execution Prevention tab in the System Properties dialog or via the command line using the bcdedit tool, specifically by running bcdedit /set {current} nx AlwaysOn, illustrating how administrators can enforce DEP system-wide, stack smashing protection (SSP) is a variant of stack canaries that adds additional security measures to protect against stack-based buffer overflows, it involves runtime checks and can detect more sophisticated attack techniques, enabling SSP in GCC can be accomplished by compiling with the -fstack-protector-strong flag, for example, gcc -o program program.c -fstack-protector-strong, demonstrating how SSP strengthens the defense against buffer overflow vulnerabilities, control flow integrity (CFI) is another advanced protection mechanism that verifies the integrity of a program's control flow graph at runtime to detect and prevent code injection attacks, implementing CFI typically involves compiler modifications and runtime instrumentation, with tools like LLVM's Control Flow Integrity Pass providing support for enforcing CFI policies, developers can integrate CFI into their software development process to bolster security, runtime exploit mitigations such as heap randomization and shadow stacks complement compile-time protections by adding additional layers of defense against buffer overflow exploits, for instance, enabling heap randomization in Linux systems can be achieved by setting the MMAP_RAND_BITS environment variable to a non-zero value before running a program susceptible to heap-based attacks, showing how runtime mitigations can be configured to enhance security, overall, buffer overflow protection mechanisms play a crucial role in safeguarding software systems from one of the most prevalent and damaging forms of cyber attacks, by combining various techniques such as stack canaries, ASLR, DEP, SSP, and CFI, organizations can significantly reduce the risk posed by buffer overflow vulnerabilities and enhance the overall security posture of their applications and systems.

Chapter 9: Network Traffic Analysis and Packet Crafting

Analyzing network traffic with Wireshark is a fundamental skill for cybersecurity professionals, as it allows for the inspection and understanding of data flows within a network, the first step in using Wireshark is to capture network packets, which can be done by selecting the appropriate network interface and starting a capture session, for example, to capture packets on interface eth0, one would use the command sudo wireshark -i eth0, demonstrating how Wireshark can be invoked from the command line with the -i flag to specify the interface, once packets are captured, they can be analyzed using Wireshark's rich set of features, such as packet filtering, protocol analysis, and packet reconstruction, filtering packets based on specific criteria can help narrow down the focus of analysis, for instance, the display filter tcp.port == 80 can be used to show only TCP packets with destination port 80, illustrating how filters can be applied to isolate relevant traffic, Wireshark's protocol analysis capabilities allow for the decoding and interpretation of various network protocols, enabling users to understand the structure and content of different types of traffic, for example, Wireshark can dissect HTTP requests and responses, DNS queries, and SMTP transactions, providing insights into the communication patterns within the network, in addition to protocol analysis, Wireshark can reconstruct higher-level data streams, such as images, documents, and audio/video streams, from captured packets, this feature is particularly useful for forensic analysis and investigating suspicious network activities, for instance, the "Follow TCP Stream" option in Wireshark allows users to reconstruct and view the entire content of a TCP connection in a single window, facilitating the analysis of application-layer protocols, beyond basic packet analysis, Wireshark offers advanced features like statistical analysis and protocol-specific expert analysis, these features can help identify anomalies, performance bottlenecks, and security issues within the network, for example, Wireshark's TCP Stream Graph tool provides visualizations of TCP connection statistics, allowing users to identify patterns and anomalies in network traffic, the protocol-specific expert analysis feature in Wireshark automatically detects and highlights potential protocol violations and errors, aiding in the identification of misconfigurations and security threats, moreover, Wireshark supports the integration of external tools and plugins, extending its functionality for specific use cases, for instance, the "tshark" command-line utility, which is part of the Wireshark suite, allows for batch processing of packet captures and automated analysis tasks, demonstrating how Wireshark can be integrated into larger automated workflows for network monitoring and security analysis, overall, Wireshark is a powerful and versatile tool for analyzing network traffic, offering a wide range of features and capabilities for investigating and troubleshooting network issues, conducting security audits, and performing forensic investigations.

Crafting and injecting packets using Scapy is a fundamental skill for network engineers and cybersecurity professionals alike, as it provides a flexible and powerful way to interact with network protocols and traffic, Scapy is a Python-based packet manipulation tool that allows users to create, send, capture, and analyze network packets programmatically, the first step in using Scapy is to install it, which can be done using the pip package manager with the command pip install scapy, illustrating how to install Scapy via the command line, once installed, users can start a Python interpreter and import Scapy's functionality with the command from scapy.all import *, demonstrating how to import Scapy's modules for packet manipulation, with Scapy, users can craft custom packets by specifying their fields and values using Python syntax, for example, to create an Ethernet frame with an IPv4 packet inside, one can use the following code snippet:

```python
Copy code
eth_pkt      =      Ether(src="00:11:22:33:44:55", dst="ff:ff:ff:ff:ff:ff")  ip_pkt  =  IP(src="192.168.1.1", dst="192.168.1.2")
```

illustrating how to create Ethernet and IP packets using Scapy's object-oriented API, users can then combine these packets and send them over the network using Scapy's send function, for instance, to send the previously created packets, one can use the following command:

python
Copy code

```
send(eth_pkt/ip_pkt)
```

showcasing how to send a packet composed of an Ethernet frame encapsulating an IPv4 packet, Scapy also supports injecting packets into the network stack of the local machine, allowing for testing and simulation of network protocols without actually sending packets over the network, for example, to inject a packet into the local network stack, one can use the following command:

python
Copy code

```
sendp(eth_pkt/ip_pkt, iface="eth0")
```

demonstrating how to inject a packet into the network stack of interface eth0, Scapy's versatility extends beyond packet creation and injection, as it also supports packet sniffing and parsing, allowing users to capture and analyze network traffic in real-time, for instance, to sniff packets on a specific interface and display their details, one can use the following command:

python
Copy code

```
sniff(iface="eth0", count=10)
```
showing how to sniff 10 packets on interface eth0 and display their contents, Scapy also provides a wide range of built-in protocols and layers, making it easy to work with various network protocols and formats, from Ethernet and IP to TCP, UDP, DNS, and beyond, for example, to create a TCP packet with custom options, one can use the following code snippet:

python

Copy code

```python
tcp_pkt = TCP(sport=1234, dport=80, flags="S", options=[('Timestamp', (123456, 0))])
```

illustrating how to create a TCP packet with SYN flag and custom TCP options using Scapy's built-in classes, in addition to its core functionality, Scapy supports scripting and automation through Python, allowing users to build complex network tools and utilities, for instance, one can write a Python script to perform network scanning, packet sniffing, or protocol fuzzing using Scapy's APIs, overall, Scapy is a powerful and versatile tool for packet manipulation and network analysis, providing Python programmers with a convenient and flexible framework for working with network protocols and traffic.

Chapter 10: Incident Response and Network Forensics

Incident response planning and preparation are essential components of any organization's cybersecurity strategy, as they enable timely and effective responses to security incidents, the first step in incident response planning is to establish an incident response team, consisting of individuals from various departments such as IT, security, legal, and management, tasked with coordinating and executing the organization's incident response efforts, establishing an incident response team can be done through formal appointments and training sessions, where team members are assigned roles and responsibilities and trained on incident response procedures and protocols, typical roles within an incident response team include incident coordinator, technical analysts, legal counsel, and public relations personnel, each with specific duties and functions during an incident, once the incident response team is in place, the next step is to develop an incident response plan (IRP), which outlines the procedures and processes for responding to security incidents, an IRP should include key elements such as incident detection and classification, escalation procedures, containment and eradication steps, recovery and restoration processes, and post-incident analysis and reporting, developing an IRP involves assessing potential threats and vulnerabilities, identifying critical assets and systems, and defining response procedures for various types of incidents, such as malware infections, data breaches, or denial-of-service attacks, the IRP should also specify communication protocols and contact information for internal and external stakeholders, including employees, customers, partners, regulators, and law enforcement agencies, ensuring clear and timely communication during an incident is crucial for managing the situation effectively and minimizing its impact, once the IRP is developed, it should be tested and validated through tabletop exercises and simulated incident scenarios, allowing the incident response team to practice their roles and procedures in a controlled environment, tabletop exercises involve simulating different types of security incidents and walking through the response process step by step, while identifying areas for improvement and refinement, these exercises help validate the effectiveness of the IRP and identify gaps or weaknesses that need to be addressed, based on the lessons learned from tabletop exercises and simulations, the IRP should be updated and refined regularly to reflect changes in the organization's infrastructure, technologies, and threat landscape, ensuring that it remains relevant and effective over time, in addition to developing an IRP, organizations should also implement proactive measures to enhance their incident response capabilities, such as deploying security monitoring and detection tools, establishing incident detection and alerting mechanisms, and conducting regular security assessments and audits, these measures help organizations detect and respond to security incidents more quickly and effectively, reducing the likelihood of successful attacks and minimizing their impact on the business, overall, incident response planning and preparation are critical components of a comprehensive cybersecurity strategy, helping organizations effectively detect, respond to, and recover from security incidents, by establishing an incident response team, developing an IRP, and implementing proactive security measures, organizations can enhance their resilience to cyber threats and better protect their assets, data, and reputation. Network forensics investigation techniques involve the systematic analysis of network traffic, logs, and other digital artifacts to identify, analyze, and mitigate security incidents, the first step in a network forensics investigation is to gather and preserve evidence, this includes capturing network packets, logs, and system images in a forensically sound manner to ensure the integrity and admissibility of the evidence in legal proceedings, packet capture tools such as tcpdump, Wireshark, or tshark can be used to capture network traffic on a specific interface or subnet, ensuring that all packets are captured and stored for later analysis, when capturing packets, it's important to use filters and capture buffers to focus on relevant traffic and avoid overwhelming the storage capacity, once the evidence is collected, the next step is to analyze the captured data to reconstruct the timeline of events and identify any suspicious or malicious activity, Wireshark is a powerful network protocol analyzer that allows forensic analysts to examine captured packets in detail, filtering, sorting, and dissecting network protocols to identify anomalies or indicators of compromise, analysts can use Wireshark's built-in filters and display options to focus on specific protocols, conversations, or traffic patterns, enabling them to quickly pinpoint potential security issues, in addition to packet analysis, network forensics investigations often involve correlating network logs and system logs to provide a comprehensive view of the incident, log analysis tools such as Splunk, ELK Stack, or Graylog can be used to aggregate, search, and analyze log data from various sources, including firewalls, intrusion detection systems, and servers, enabling analysts to identify patterns, trends, and anomalies indicative of unauthorized activity, network forensics investigations also rely on open-source intelligence (OSINT) and threat intelligence feeds to enrich and contextualize the findings, OSINT sources such as public databases, social media platforms, and internet archives can provide valuable insights into the attackers' tactics, techniques, and infrastructure, enabling analysts to attribute the activity to specific threat actors or groups, threat intelligence feeds from commercial vendors or industry groups can provide real-time information on emerging threats, vulnerabilities, and attack campaigns, helping organizations proactively defend against cyber threats, as part of the investigation process, forensic analysts may also perform memory analysis on compromised systems to identify malware, rootkits, or other malicious code that may be running in memory, memory forensics tools such as Volatility or Rekall can be used to extract and analyze volatile data from RAM dumps, providing insights into the runtime behavior of the malware and its impact on the system, finally, network forensics investigations culminate in the generation of a detailed report documenting the findings, analysis, and recommendations, the report should include a summary of the incident, a timeline of events, an analysis of the attack vectors and tactics used, and recommendations for mitigating the risk and improving the organization's security posture, overall, network forensics investigation techniques play a crucial role in identifying and mitigating security incidents, enabling organizations to respond effectively to cyber threats and protect their assets, data, and reputation.

BOOK 4
PENTEST+ EXAM PASS
EXPERT INSIGHTS AND REAL-WORLD SCENARIOS

ROB BOTWRIGHT

Chapter 1: Advanced Social Engineering Tactics

Psychological manipulation techniques encompass a wide array of tactics used to influence and control individuals' thoughts, emotions, and behaviors, one common technique is gaslighting, where the manipulator distorts the victim's perception of reality to make them doubt their own sanity or judgment, gaslighting often involves denying or trivializing the victim's experiences, emotions, or concerns, causing them to question their memory, perception, or sanity, for example, an abusive partner may repeatedly tell their victim that they're imagining things or overreacting to situations, undermining their confidence and self-esteem, another manipulation technique is guilt-tripping, where the manipulator uses guilt or shame to manipulate the victim into doing what they want, this can involve making the victim feel responsible for the manipulator's emotions, actions, or well-being, creating a sense of obligation or indebtedness, for instance, a parent may guilt-trip their child into compliance by saying things like "after all I've done for you, you can't even do this one thing for me?", exploiting the child's sense of duty and loyalty, manipulation can also involve emotional blackmail, where the manipulator threatens to withhold love, approval, or support unless the victim complies with their demands, this can create a sense of fear, obligation, or dependency, making it difficult for the victim to assert their own needs or boundaries, an example of emotional blackmail is a boss threatening to fire an employee if they don't work overtime, using the employee's fear of losing their job to manipulate them into sacrificing their personal time or well-being, another manipulation technique is love bombing, where the manipulator showers the victim with affection, attention, and praise to gain their trust and loyalty, this can create a strong emotional bond and make the victim more susceptible to manipulation, for instance, a romantic partner may inundate their significant other with compliments, gifts, and gestures of affection in the early stages of a relationship, making it harder for the victim to see any red flags or warning signs of abuse, manipulation can also involve isolating the victim from their support network, making them more dependent on the manipulator for validation, validation, and guidance, for example, an abusive partner may discourage their victim from spending time with friends or family, undermining their social connections and weakening their support system, ultimately making them easier to control, furthermore, manipulation can exploit cognitive biases and heuristics to influence decision-making and perception, for instance, confirmation bias can lead individuals to seek out information that confirms their preconceived beliefs while ignoring or dismissing contradictory evidence, manipulators can exploit this bias by selectively presenting information that supports their agenda, reinforcing the victim's existing beliefs and biases, similarly, anchoring bias can influence individuals' judgments by relying too heavily on the first piece of information they encounter, manipulators can exploit this bias by framing the discussion or negotiation in a way that favors their position, shaping the victim's perception of what's reasonable or acceptable, moreover, manipulation can exploit the fear of missing out (FOMO) to pressure individuals into making decisions or taking actions they wouldn't otherwise consider, for example, a salesperson may create a sense of urgency or scarcity to encourage customers to make impulsive purchases, playing on their fear of missing out on a limited-time offer or exclusive deal, manipulation can also exploit social proof, where individuals look to others' behavior or opinions for guidance on how to act or think, manipulators can leverage social proof by presenting themselves as popular, successful, or authoritative figures, influencing the victim to follow their lead or conform to their expectations, overall, psychological manipulation techniques are pervasive and can have profound effects on individuals' mental, emotional, and social well-being, recognizing these tactics and learning how to protect oneself from manipulation is essential for maintaining healthy relationships and personal autonomy.

Social engineering techniques play a pivotal role in phishing and vishing attacks, where attackers exploit human psychology and trust to deceive individuals into divulging sensitive information or performing actions that compromise their security, in phishing attacks, perpetrators typically impersonate legitimate entities, such as banks, social media platforms, or online retailers, to trick recipients into clicking on malicious links or providing confidential information, one common phishing tactic involves sending deceptive emails that appear to originate from trusted sources, prompting recipients to click on malicious links or download malicious attachments, for example, an attacker may craft an email impersonating a bank, claiming that the recipient's account has been compromised and urging them to click on a link to verify their credentials, once the victim clicks on the link and enters their login credentials, the attacker can harvest this information for unauthorized access to the victim's account, phishing attacks can also exploit psychological triggers, such as urgency or curiosity, to manipulate recipients into taking immediate action without questioning the legitimacy of the request, for instance, an email claiming that the recipient has won a prize or that their account will be suspended unless they take immediate action can prompt impulsive responses, increasing the likelihood of falling victim to the scam, furthermore, vishing attacks leverage voice communication to deceive individuals, vishing, short for "voice phishing," typically involves automated phone calls or pre-recorded messages that impersonate legitimate organizations, such as banks or government agencies, to trick recipients into disclosing sensitive information or transferring funds, for example, a vishing scam may involve a recorded message claiming to be from a bank, informing the recipient that their account has been compromised and instructing them to press a key to speak with a representative, once the victim engages with the call, they may be prompted to provide personal information or input sensitive account details, which the attacker can then exploit for fraudulent purposes, vishing attacks can also involve live callers who impersonate customer service representatives or technical support personnel to gain the victim's trust and coax them into revealing sensitive information, for example, an attacker posing as a tech support agent may contact the victim and claim that their computer has been infected with malware, instructing them to download remote access software to "fix" the problem, once the victim grants the attacker remote access to their device, the attacker can install malicious software or steal sensitive data, it's essential for individuals and organizations to remain vigilant and adopt defensive measures to protect against phishing and vishing attacks, this includes implementing robust email filtering and anti-phishing solutions to detect and block malicious emails, providing regular security awareness training to educate users about the dangers of social engineering tactics and how to recognize phishing attempts, encouraging employees to verify the legitimacy of unexpected requests for sensitive information or financial transactions, such as by contacting the purported sender through official channels or visiting their website directly, implementing multi-factor authentication (MFA) to add an extra layer of security to user accounts, requiring users to provide additional verification, such as a one-time code sent to their mobile device, before accessing sensitive data or performing certain actions, regularly monitoring network traffic and user activity for signs of unauthorized access or suspicious behavior, and promptly reporting any suspected phishing or vishing attempts to the appropriate authorities or IT security personnel for investigation and remediation, by taking proactive steps to defend against social engineering attacks, individuals and organizations can mitigate the risk of falling victim to these insidious threats and safeguard their sensitive information and assets from exploitation.

Chapter 2: Advanced Persistent Threats (APTs) Analysis

APT attacks, or Advanced Persistent Threats, represent some of the most sophisticated and persistent cyber threats faced by organizations today, these attacks are typically launched by highly skilled and well-funded threat actors, such as nation-state sponsored groups or organized cybercriminal syndicates, with the primary goal of stealing sensitive information, disrupting operations, or causing financial harm, APT attackers employ a variety of tactics, techniques, and procedures (TTPs) to infiltrate target networks, evade detection, and maintain long-term access, one common characteristic of APT attacks is their stealthy and persistent nature, APT attackers often conduct extensive reconnaissance to gather intelligence about their targets, including information about network infrastructure, security defenses, and potential vulnerabilities, this reconnaissance phase may involve scanning for open ports and services, enumerating active directory objects, and collecting publicly available information from social media platforms, blogs, or company websites, armed with this reconnaissance data, attackers can identify potential entry points and develop tailored attack strategies to exploit weaknesses in the target's defenses, APT attackers frequently use spear phishing emails as an initial vector for infiltration, spear phishing involves sending highly targeted emails to specific individuals within an organization, impersonating trusted senders or leveraging social engineering tactics to trick recipients into opening malicious attachments or clicking on malicious links, once an unsuspecting user interacts with the malicious payload, the attacker can establish a foothold within the target network and begin escalating privileges to gain access to sensitive systems and data, APT attackers often leverage zero-day exploits or other advanced techniques to bypass security controls and remain undetected within the target environment, zero-day exploits are previously unknown vulnerabilities in software or hardware that have not yet been patched by the vendor, by exploiting these vulnerabilities, attackers can gain unauthorized access to systems or execute arbitrary code with elevated privileges, enabling them to install backdoors, exfiltrate data, or deploy additional malware payloads, APT attackers also employ sophisticated evasion techniques to avoid detection by security monitoring tools and forensic investigators, this may include using encryption and obfuscation to conceal malicious payloads, leveraging legitimate tools and protocols for command and control communication, and employing anti-forensic techniques to erase evidence of their presence on compromised systems, one of the most challenging aspects of defending against APT attacks is their adaptability and persistence, APT attackers are adept at evolving their tactics in response to changes in the threat landscape and security posture of their targets, they may modify their malware, infrastructure, or TTPs to bypass newly implemented security controls or exploit emerging vulnerabilities, as such, organizations must adopt a proactive and multi-layered approach to cybersecurity, including robust threat intelligence capabilities, continuous monitoring and analysis of network traffic and user behavior, and regular security awareness training for employees, in addition, organizations should implement strong access controls, segment networks to limit the impact of a successful breach, and regularly patch and update software to mitigate the risk of exploitation by known vulnerabilities, by taking these proactive measures and remaining vigilant against emerging threats, organizations can enhance their resilience to APT attacks and better protect their critical assets and information from compromise. APT detection and mitigation strategies are crucial components of an organization's cybersecurity posture, given the stealthy and persistent nature of APT attacks, organizations must deploy a combination of proactive measures and reactive controls to detect and mitigate these threats effectively, one proactive approach to APT detection is the implementation of robust network monitoring and anomaly detection systems, these systems continuously analyze network traffic, user behavior, and system activity to identify suspicious patterns or deviations from normal behavior, for example, network intrusion detection systems (NIDS) can monitor network traffic for known attack signatures or unusual traffic patterns indicative of APT activity, similarly, host-based intrusion detection systems (HIDS) can monitor individual endpoints for signs of compromise, such as unauthorized access attempts or anomalous process behavior, in addition to intrusion detection, organizations should also implement security information and event management (SIEM) solutions to aggregate and correlate security events from across the network, SIEM platforms can provide real-time visibility into potential security incidents, enabling security analysts to quickly investigate and respond to threats, another proactive measure for APT detection is the implementation of threat intelligence feeds and indicators of compromise (IOCs), threat intelligence feeds provide organizations with timely and relevant information about emerging threats, including known APT campaigns, malware variants, and attack techniques, by integrating threat intelligence feeds into their security infrastructure, organizations can proactively block malicious traffic, update security controls, and prioritize incident response efforts, furthermore, organizations can deploy network segmentation and access controls to limit the lateral movement of APT attackers within their networks, network segmentation involves dividing the network into smaller, isolated segments or zones, each with its own security policies and access controls, by restricting lateral movement between network segments, organizations can contain APT attackers and prevent them from accessing critical systems and data, additionally, organizations should conduct regular security assessments and penetration tests to identify and remediate vulnerabilities before they can be exploited by APT attackers, penetration testing involves simulating real-world attack scenarios to assess the security posture of an organization's systems and networks, during a penetration test, security professionals attempt to exploit known vulnerabilities or misconfigurations to gain unauthorized access to systems or data, by identifying and fixing these vulnerabilities, organizations can reduce their exposure to APT attacks, despite these proactive measures, organizations must also be prepared to respond to APT attacks that successfully breach their defenses, this requires the development and implementation of an effective incident response plan, an incident response plan outlines the steps and procedures for detecting, containing, and mitigating security incidents, including APT attacks, it should define roles and responsibilities for incident response team members, establish communication channels for reporting and escalating incidents, and outline the steps for restoring normal operations after an incident, in addition to technical controls, organizations must also focus on security awareness and training for employees, human error remains one of the most significant factors contributing to successful APT attacks, phishing emails, social engineering, and other tactics are commonly used by APT attackers to gain a foothold within target organizations, by educating employees about the risks of APT attacks and providing training on how to recognize and report suspicious activity, organizations can reduce the likelihood of successful APT attacks, In summary, APT detection and mitigation require a multi-layered approach that combines proactive measures, such as network monitoring, threat intelligence, and access controls, with reactive controls, such as incident response planning and security awareness training, by implementing these strategies, organizations can better defend against APT attacks and protect their critical assets and information from compromise.

Chapter 3: Exploiting IoT Devices and Industrial Control Systems

Vulnerabilities in IoT devices and Industrial Control Systems (ICS) pose significant risks to both individuals and organizations, as the number of connected devices continues to grow rapidly, so too does the attack surface for potential exploitation, IoT devices, such as smart home appliances, wearables, and connected medical devices, often lack robust security controls, making them vulnerable to a wide range of attacks, one common vulnerability in IoT devices is the use of default or hard-coded credentials, many manufacturers ship devices with default usernames and passwords that are rarely changed by end-users, attackers can exploit these default credentials to gain unauthorized access to IoT devices and compromise them, for example, an attacker could remotely access a smart thermostat using default credentials and manipulate the temperature settings to disrupt HVAC operations or cause physical damage, another common vulnerability in IoT devices is insecure firmware or software, many IoT devices run outdated or unpatched software that contains known security vulnerabilities, attackers can exploit these vulnerabilities to execute arbitrary code, escalate privileges, or gain persistent access to the device, for example, a vulnerability in the firmware of a network-connected security camera could allow an attacker to intercept video feeds or launch denial-of-service attacks against other devices on the network, in addition to vulnerabilities in individual devices, IoT ecosystems often lack proper network segmentation and access controls, allowing attackers to move laterally within the network and compromise additional devices, for example, an attacker who gains access to a vulnerable smart home hub could use it as a pivot point to compromise other devices on the same network, including computers, smartphones, and connected appliances, furthermore, IoT devices often lack secure update mechanisms, making it difficult for manufacturers to patch vulnerabilities in deployed devices, this can leave devices vulnerable to exploitation for extended periods, even after patches or security updates are available, for example, a vulnerability in the firmware of a smart light bulb may go unpatched for months or even years, exposing the device to potential exploitation by attackers, industrial control systems (ICS), which are used to monitor and control critical infrastructure such as power plants, water treatment facilities, and manufacturing plants, are also susceptible to vulnerabilities, attacks against ICS can have serious consequences, including disruptions to essential services, environmental damage, and loss of life, one common vulnerability in ICS is the lack of segmentation between operational technology (OT) networks and enterprise IT networks, many organizations connect their ICS directly to the internet or to corporate networks, increasing the risk of unauthorized access and exploitation, for example, an attacker who gains access to an organization's corporate network could use it to pivot into the OT network and manipulate industrial processes or disrupt critical operations, another common vulnerability in ICS is the use of legacy or unsupported software, many ICS rely on outdated operating systems, applications, and protocols that are no longer supported by vendors, these legacy systems are often riddled with known vulnerabilities that attackers can exploit to gain unauthorized access or disrupt operations, for example, the use of outdated versions of Windows or Linux in ICS environments can expose them to vulnerabilities such as EternalBlue or Heartbleed, which have been exploited in high-profile cyber attacks, in addition to software vulnerabilities, ICS are also susceptible to physical attacks, such as tampering, sabotage, or theft, attackers may attempt to physically access ICS equipment to install malicious hardware or manipulate control systems, for example, an attacker could insert a rogue device into an industrial control network to intercept or modify data packets, compromise control systems, or cause physical damage to equipment, addressing vulnerabilities in IoT devices and ICS requires a multi-faceted approach that includes both technical controls and organizational policies, organizations should implement security best practices such as network segmentation, access controls, secure update mechanisms, and regular security assessments to identify and remediate vulnerabilities in IoT devices and ICS, furthermore, manufacturers should prioritize security throughout the entire product lifecycle, from design and development to deployment and maintenance, by building security into IoT devices and ICS from the ground up, manufacturers can reduce the risk of vulnerabilities and improve the overall security posture of connected systems, In summary, vulnerabilities in IoT devices and ICS pose significant risks to individuals, organizations, and society as a whole, addressing these vulnerabilities requires a collaborative effort involving manufacturers, vendors, regulators, and end-users to develop and implement effective security controls and best practices.

Exploiting IoT (Internet of Things) and ICS (Industrial Control Systems) systems requires a deep understanding of their architecture, vulnerabilities, and potential attack vectors, IoT devices and ICS systems are often interconnected and integrated into critical infrastructure, making them attractive targets for attackers seeking to disrupt operations, steal sensitive information, or cause physical damage, one common technique for exploiting IoT devices is to identify and exploit vulnerabilities in their firmware or software, attackers may use tools such as Shodan or Nmap to scan the internet for vulnerable devices and services, for example, an attacker could use the following Nmap command to scan a range of IP addresses for devices running the Telnet service: nmap -p 23 192.168.1.0/24, once a vulnerable device is identified, attackers may attempt to exploit known vulnerabilities to gain unauthorized access or execute arbitrary code, for example, an attacker could use the Telnet service to login to a vulnerable IoT device using default credentials and then execute commands to take control of the device, another technique for exploiting IoT devices is to intercept and manipulate their communication protocols, many IoT devices communicate over insecure protocols such as HTTP, MQTT, or CoAP, attackers may use tools such as Wireshark or tcpdump to capture and analyze network traffic between IoT devices and their associated servers or gateways, for example, an attacker could use the following tcpdump command to capture HTTP traffic on a network interface: tcpdump -i eth0 -s 0 -w capture.pcap port 80, once network traffic has been captured, attackers may attempt to identify sensitive information such as passwords, API keys, or device identifiers, attackers may also attempt to inject malicious payloads into network traffic to exploit vulnerabilities in IoT devices or compromise their associated servers or gateways, for example, an attacker could use the following command to inject a malicious payload into an HTTP request using the curl utility: curl -X POST -d '<?php system($_GET["cmd"]); ?>' http://vulnerable-device/api, in addition to exploiting vulnerabilities in IoT devices themselves, attackers may also target the infrastructure that supports them, such as cloud servers, mobile apps, or web portals, for example, an attacker could exploit a vulnerability in a cloud server hosting an IoT device's backend infrastructure to gain unauthorized access to sensitive data or control the device remotely, attackers may also exploit vulnerabilities in mobile apps or web portals used to manage IoT devices to steal user credentials or compromise devices, for example, an attacker could use a phishing email to trick a user into clicking on a malicious link that exploits a vulnerability in a mobile app to steal their login credentials, once access to an IoT device or ICS system has been gained, attackers may attempt to escalate their privileges or move laterally within the network to compromise additional devices or systems, for example, an attacker who gains access to an IoT device running Linux may attempt to escalate their privileges by exploiting a known vulnerability in the Linux kernel, such as Dirty COW, to gain root access, attackers may also use tools such as Metasploit or PowerShell Empire to automate the process of escalating privileges and moving laterally within a network, for example, an attacker could use the following Metasploit command to exploit a vulnerability in a Windows system and gain a Meterpreter shell: use exploit/windows/local/ms16_032_secondary_logon _handle_privesc, In summary, exploiting IoT and ICS systems requires a combination of technical skills, knowledge of vulnerabilities, and understanding of the underlying infrastructure, attackers may use a variety of techniques to identify and exploit vulnerabilities in IoT devices and associated infrastructure, organizations must implement robust security controls and practices to protect against these threats and minimize the risk of compromise or disruption.

Chapter 4: Advanced Malware Analysis and Reverse Engineering

Dynamic and static malware analysis techniques are essential methodologies employed by cybersecurity professionals to understand the behavior, structure, and impact of malicious software. Static analysis involves examining the code and structure of malware without executing it, while dynamic analysis involves observing the behavior of malware in a controlled environment. Static analysis techniques include examining file properties, analyzing strings and code patterns, and using disassemblers and decompilers to understand the functionality of the malware. For example, tools like IDA Pro or Ghidra can be used to disassemble and analyze the binary code of malware samples to identify malicious functions and behaviors. Additionally, static analysis involves examining the metadata and digital signatures of files to detect signs of tampering or malicious intent. Command-line tools like file and strings can provide valuable insights into the nature of a file, while antivirus scanners can detect known malware signatures. On the other hand, dynamic analysis involves executing malware in a controlled environment, such as a sandbox or virtual machine, to observe its behavior and interactions with the system. Tools like Cuckoo Sandbox or FireEye's FLARE VM can automate the process of dynamic analysis by executing malware samples in isolated environments and monitoring their behavior. During dynamic analysis, analysts can observe the actions taken by malware, such as file system modifications, network communications, and registry changes, to understand its capabilities and objectives. For instance, network monitoring tools like Wireshark can capture and analyze network traffic generated by malware, while process monitoring tools like Process Monitor can track system calls and process activity. Additionally, memory analysis tools like Volatility can be used to examine the memory of an infected system to identify malware artifacts and indicators of compromise. By combining static and dynamic analysis techniques, cybersecurity professionals can gain a comprehensive understanding of malware behavior, characteristics, and impact on systems and networks. This holistic approach enables organizations to develop effective strategies for detecting, mitigating, and responding to malware threats. Moreover, by leveraging threat intelligence feeds and malware repositories, analysts can correlate their findings with known malware families and attack patterns to identify the origin and purpose of malicious software. Additionally, sandbox evasion techniques such as anti-VM detection, time-based triggers, and anti-analysis tricks may require analysts to employ advanced evasion detection techniques to accurately analyze malware samples. Furthermore, behavioral analysis involves monitoring the execution flow of malware to identify patterns and anomalies that may indicate malicious intent. By analyzing the behavior of malware in a controlled environment, analysts can identify indicators of compromise (IOCs) and develop signatures or heuristics to detect similar threats in the future. Finally, static and dynamic analysis techniques are complemented by reverse engineering, which involves analyzing the inner workings of malware to understand its functionality and uncover vulnerabilities that can be exploited for detection or mitigation purposes. Through continuous refinement and improvement of malware analysis techniques, cybersecurity professionals can stay ahead of evolving threats and protect organizations from the impact of malicious software.

Advanced reverse engineering methods are indispensable techniques utilized by cybersecurity professionals to delve deep into the inner workings of software, firmware, and hardware to uncover hidden functionalities, vulnerabilities, and potential attack vectors. These techniques go beyond basic static and dynamic analysis approaches and involve sophisticated methodologies aimed at understanding complex systems and uncovering intricate details obscured by obfuscation, encryption, or anti-reverse engineering mechanisms. One such method is binary code analysis, which involves disassembling executable files or firmware to examine the low-level assembly instructions and control flow of the program. Tools like IDA Pro, Binary Ninja, or Ghidra enable analysts to navigate through the binary code, identify function calls, and reconstruct the high-level logic of the software. Another advanced technique is code emulation, which involves creating a virtual environment to execute and analyze binary code without running it on physical hardware. Tools like QEMU or Unicorn Engine provide emulation capabilities, allowing analysts to observe the behavior of malware or suspicious binaries in a controlled environment while monitoring system interactions and resource usage. Furthermore, advanced reverse engineering often involves the use of sophisticated debugging techniques to dynamically analyze the behavior of software during runtime. Debuggers like GDB or WinDbg enable analysts to set breakpoints, inspect memory, and trace program execution to understand how software interacts with the system and identify potential vulnerabilities or malicious behavior. Additionally, memory forensics plays a crucial role in advanced reverse engineering by enabling analysts to analyze the contents of a system's memory to uncover artifacts left behind by malicious software or attackers. Tools like Volatility or Rekall provide capabilities for extracting and analyzing memory dumps, allowing analysts to identify malware processes, injected code, and other anomalous behavior indicative of a compromise. Moreover, advanced reverse engineering methods often involve the use of advanced obfuscation and anti-analysis techniques to thwart traditional analysis approaches. For instance, malware authors may employ code obfuscation, encryption, or packing techniques to make analysis more challenging. To overcome these obstacles, analysts may use deobfuscation tools or custom scripts to unravel the obfuscated code and reveal its true functionality. Additionally, advanced reverse engineering may involve hardware reverse engineering techniques aimed at understanding the inner workings of embedded systems, IoT devices, or hardware security modules. This can include techniques such as chip decapsulation, PCB reverse engineering, or side-channel analysis to uncover vulnerabilities or backdoors hidden within the hardware. Furthermore, advanced reverse engineering methods often require a deep understanding of computer architecture, operating systems, and network protocols to effectively analyze complex software systems and uncover subtle vulnerabilities or attack vectors. By combining expertise in software engineering, computer science, and cybersecurity, analysts can develop comprehensive reverse engineering strategies to dissect and understand even the most sophisticated software and hardware systems. Additionally, collaboration and knowledge sharing within the cybersecurity community play a crucial role in advancing reverse engineering methods and staying ahead of emerging threats. Through continuous research, experimentation, and innovation, cybersecurity professionals can develop new tools, techniques, and methodologies to tackle the challenges posed by evolving malware, exploits, and attack techniques. Ultimately, advanced reverse engineering methods empower organizations to identify and mitigate security risks, protect critical assets, and safeguard against cyber threats in an increasingly complex and interconnected digital landscape.

Chapter 5: Insider Threat Detection and Mitigation

Insider threat indicators and behavior analysis are critical components of cybersecurity strategies aimed at detecting and mitigating risks posed by individuals with authorized access to an organization's systems, networks, or data who may intentionally or unintentionally cause harm or disclose sensitive information. These threats can manifest in various forms, including data exfiltration, sabotage, espionage, or fraud, and may be perpetrated by employees, contractors, or trusted third parties. To effectively detect insider threats, organizations rely on advanced monitoring and analysis techniques to identify suspicious behaviors, anomalies, or deviations from normal patterns of activity. One common indicator of insider threats is unusual access patterns, such as accessing sensitive files or systems outside of regular working hours or accessing resources unrelated to the individual's job responsibilities. Monitoring user authentication and access logs using tools like Splunk or ELK Stack can help identify unauthorized access attempts or suspicious login activity that may indicate insider threats. Additionally, changes in behavior or performance may serve as red flags for insider threats, such as sudden changes in work patterns, increased use of removable storage devices, or attempts to bypass security controls. Behavioral analytics tools like Darktrace or User and Entity Behavior Analytics (UEBA) platforms can analyze user activity logs and network traffic to identify abnormal behaviors indicative of insider threats. Moreover, indicators of insider threats may also include disgruntled employees, individuals experiencing financial difficulties, or those who exhibit signs of stress or emotional instability. Human resources departments can play a crucial role in identifying and addressing these issues through employee monitoring, performance evaluations, and regular communication to detect potential insider threats early on. Furthermore, insider threats may involve the unauthorized disclosure of sensitive information or intellectual property to external parties, either intentionally or unintentionally. Monitoring outbound network traffic and data transfers using data loss prevention (DLP) solutions like Symantec DLP or McAfee DLP can help organizations detect and prevent unauthorized data exfiltration attempts by insiders. Additionally, analyzing email communications and file transfers for sensitive keywords or patterns indicative of data leakage can help organizations identify and mitigate insider threats before they cause significant damage. Furthermore, insider threats may exploit vulnerabilities in privileged access to systems or data to carry out malicious activities. Monitoring privileged user accounts and implementing least privilege principles can help organizations limit the potential impact of insider threats by restricting access to sensitive resources only to authorized individuals on a need-to-know basis. Privileged access management (PAM) solutions like CyberArk or BeyondTrust provide capabilities for managing, monitoring, and controlling access to privileged accounts and systems to prevent insider threats. Additionally, insider threats may involve the misuse of credentials or access rights to gain unauthorized access to systems, networks, or data. Regularly auditing user accounts, permissions, and entitlements using tools like Microsoft Active Directory or LDAP can help organizations identify and remediate unauthorized access or suspicious activities by insiders. Moreover, insider threats may exploit vulnerabilities in applications or systems to carry out attacks, such as installing malware, backdoors, or remote access tools to facilitate unauthorized access or data exfiltration. Conducting regular vulnerability assessments and penetration testing using tools like Nessus or Metasploit can help organizations identify and remediate security weaknesses before they are exploited by insiders or external attackers. Additionally, implementing endpoint security solutions like antivirus, intrusion detection/prevention systems (IDS/IPS), and endpoint detection and response (EDR) platforms can help organizations detect and respond to insider threats in real-time by monitoring endpoints for signs of malicious activity or unauthorized access. Furthermore, insider threats may involve the theft or misuse of sensitive information or intellectual property for personal gain or competitive advantage. Implementing data encryption, access controls, and data classification policies can help organizations protect sensitive information from insider threats by limiting access to authorized individuals and preventing unauthorized disclosure or misuse. Additionally, establishing clear policies and procedures for handling sensitive information, conducting regular security awareness training for employees, and enforcing strict data protection measures can help organizations mitigate the risk of insider threats and safeguard their critical assets. Overall, detecting and mitigating insider threats requires a multi-layered approach that combines technical controls, user monitoring, policy enforcement, and employee education to identify and respond to potential threats effectively. By implementing proactive measures and leveraging advanced analytics and monitoring capabilities, organizations can better protect themselves against insider threats and minimize the risk of data breaches, financial losses, and reputational damage.

Chapter 6: Digital Forensics and Incident Response Planning

The digital forensics investigation process is a systematic approach used to collect, preserve, analyze, and present digital evidence in a legal context to uncover the truth behind cyber incidents and criminal activities. This process typically consists of several key phases, each of which plays a crucial role in the successful resolution of digital investigations. The first phase of the digital forensics investigation process is identification and planning, where investigators gather information about the incident, define the scope of the investigation, and develop a comprehensive plan to guide their efforts. This may involve identifying key stakeholders, determining the legal and regulatory requirements, and establishing clear objectives and timelines for the investigation. Once the investigation plan is in place, the next phase is evidence acquisition, where investigators collect and preserve digital evidence relevant to the case. This may include seizing computers, mobile devices, servers, network logs, and other electronic devices, as well as making forensic copies of data to ensure its integrity and authenticity. Tools like FTK Imager or dd command in Linux can be used to create forensic images of storage devices, while chain of custody procedures and documentation are followed to maintain the integrity of the evidence throughout the investigation. With the evidence collected and preserved, the next phase is analysis, where investigators examine the digital evidence to identify relevant artifacts, patterns, and anomalies that may help uncover the truth behind the incident. This may involve using forensic software tools like EnCase or Autopsy to analyze file systems, registry entries, email communications, network traffic, and other sources of digital evidence for signs of malicious activity or unauthorized access. Additionally, investigators may use data recovery techniques to retrieve deleted files or recover overwritten data, as well as keyword searching and data carving techniques to identify and extract specific information from large datasets. As the analysis phase progresses, investigators document their findings and prepare reports detailing their methods, observations, and conclusions, which may be used to support legal proceedings or other investigative efforts. Finally, the last phase of the digital forensics investigation process is presentation, where investigators present their findings and conclusions to relevant stakeholders, such as law enforcement agencies, prosecutors, or corporate management. This may involve preparing formal reports, providing expert testimony in court, or presenting findings in a clear and understandable manner to non-technical audiences. Throughout the entire investigation process, adherence to best practices, standards, and legal requirements is essential to ensure the integrity, reliability, and admissibility of digital evidence in a court of law. This includes following established forensic methodologies, maintaining proper documentation and chain of custody procedures, and respecting individuals' privacy rights and due process protections. Moreover, collaboration and communication among investigators, legal counsel, and other stakeholders are key to the success of digital forensics investigations, ensuring that all relevant information is considered and that investigative efforts are conducted in a timely and efficient manner. By following a systematic and rigorous approach to digital forensics investigations, organizations can effectively uncover the truth behind cyber incidents and criminal activities, hold perpetrators accountable for their actions, and mitigate the risk of future incidents. Developing an effective incident response plan is crucial for organizations to mitigate the impact of cybersecurity incidents and ensure business continuity. The incident response plan outlines the procedures and guidelines that an organization must follow when responding to security incidents, such as data breaches, malware infections, or unauthorized access attempts. The first step in developing an incident response plan is to establish a dedicated incident response team comprised of individuals with the necessary technical expertise and authority to coordinate and execute the response efforts. This team should include representatives from various departments, including IT, security, legal, human resources, and executive management, to ensure that all aspects of the response are covered. Once the incident response team is formed, the next step is to conduct a thorough risk assessment to identify potential threats and vulnerabilities that could impact the organization's systems and data. This assessment should consider factors such as the organization's industry, size, geographic location, regulatory requirements, and the value of its assets. Tools like Nmap or Nessus can be used to scan the network for vulnerabilities and assess the overall security posture of the organization's infrastructure. Based on the findings of the risk assessment, the incident response team can then develop a comprehensive incident response plan that outlines the procedures and protocols for detecting, analyzing, containing, eradicating, and recovering from security incidents. This plan should include specific steps for identifying and categorizing incidents based on their severity, as well as the roles and responsibilities of each member of the incident response team. Moreover, it should define the communication channels and escalation procedures for notifying relevant stakeholders, such as senior management, legal counsel, law enforcement agencies, and regulatory authorities, in the event of a security incident. Additionally, the incident response plan should specify the tools, technologies, and resources that will be used to facilitate the response efforts, such as intrusion detection systems, security information and event management (SIEM) platforms, and forensic analysis tools. It is essential to regularly review and update the incident response plan to ensure that it remains effective in addressing emerging threats and evolving business requirements. This may involve conducting tabletop exercises or simulated incident response drills to test the plan's effectiveness and identify any gaps or weaknesses that need to be addressed. Furthermore, organizations should establish procedures for post-incident analysis and lessons learned sessions to identify opportunities for improvement and refine their incident response capabilities over time. By developing and implementing an effective incident response plan, organizations can minimize the impact of security incidents, reduce the likelihood of data breaches and other cyber threats, and maintain the trust and confidence of their customers, partners, and stakeholders.

Chapter 7: Cyber Threat Intelligence and Information Sharing

Cyber threat intelligence gathering and analysis is a critical process in modern cybersecurity operations, aimed at identifying, assessing, and mitigating potential threats to an organization's digital assets. This process involves collecting, analyzing, and disseminating information about cyber threats, including malware, vulnerabilities, hacking techniques, and threat actors, to support decision-making and improve the organization's security posture. One of the key components of cyber threat intelligence gathering is the collection of data from various sources, both internal and external. Internal sources may include security logs, network traffic data, system logs, and incident reports, while external sources may include open-source intelligence (OSINT), threat intelligence feeds, security blogs, forums, and social media platforms. Tools such as Snort, Suricata, and Bro can be used to monitor network traffic and detect potential threats in real-time, while SIEM platforms like Splunk or ELK Stack can be used to aggregate, correlate, and analyze log data from various sources. Once the data is collected, it must be analyzed to identify patterns, trends, and indicators of compromise (IOCs) that may indicate a potential threat. This analysis may involve identifying commonalities among different incidents, correlating events to uncover hidden relationships, and prioritizing threats based on their severity and potential impact on the organization. Threat intelligence platforms (TIPs) such as ThreatConnect, Anomali, and Recorded Future can be used to automate the collection, analysis, and dissemination of threat intelligence data, enabling organizations to more effectively identify and respond to emerging threats. Additionally, threat intelligence analysts may use specialized tools and techniques to conduct more in-depth analysis, such as reverse engineering malware samples, analyzing phishing emails, or tracking threat actors' activities on the dark web. Moreover, threat intelligence analysts may also engage in threat hunting activities, proactively searching for signs of malicious activity within the organization's network and systems. This may involve using tools like YARA or Snort rules to search for specific patterns or signatures associated with known threats, as well as conducting manual investigations to identify anomalous behavior or indicators of compromise. Once the analysis is complete, the findings must be disseminated to relevant stakeholders within the organization, such as security operations teams, incident response teams, and executive management. This may involve creating reports, briefings, or threat bulletins that summarize the key findings, potential impact, and recommended actions to mitigate the identified threats. Additionally, threat intelligence sharing and collaboration with other organizations, industry groups, government agencies, and cybersecurity vendors can help organizations gain access to additional threat intelligence data and improve their overall situational awareness. Finally, it is essential to continually monitor and update the organization's cyber threat intelligence program to ensure that it remains effective in addressing emerging threats and evolving security challenges. This may involve regularly reviewing and updating threat intelligence feeds, refining analysis techniques, and adapting processes and procedures based on lessons learned from past incidents. By establishing a robust cyber threat intelligence gathering and analysis program, organizations can enhance their ability to detect, respond to, and mitigate cyber threats effectively, thereby reducing the risk of data breaches, financial losses, and reputational damage.

Information sharing in cybersecurity is vital for organizations to effectively defend against evolving cyber threats, collaborate with industry peers, and enhance overall security posture. Sharing information about cyber threats, vulnerabilities, and best practices allows organizations to collectively learn from each other's experiences, strengthen their defenses, and respond more efficiently to emerging threats. One of the primary benefits of information sharing is the ability to gain insights into the latest cyber threats and attack techniques. By exchanging threat intelligence data with other organizations, cybersecurity professionals can stay informed about new malware strains, zero-day vulnerabilities, and emerging attack trends, enabling them to better anticipate and mitigate potential threats to their own networks and systems. Moreover, information sharing enables organizations to leverage collective knowledge and expertise to improve their cybersecurity defenses. By collaborating with industry peers, government agencies, and cybersecurity vendors, organizations can gain access to a broader range of threat intelligence data, analytical tools, and mitigation strategies that they may not have access to individually. This collaborative approach allows organizations to benefit from shared resources, expertise, and insights, ultimately strengthening their ability to detect, prevent, and respond to cyber threats effectively. Furthermore, information sharing fosters a sense of community and cooperation within the cybersecurity industry. By participating in information-sharing forums, threat intelligence sharing platforms, and industry working groups, cybersecurity professionals can build relationships, establish trust, and exchange valuable insights with their peers. This collaborative environment promotes greater transparency, accountability, and coordination among organizations, leading to more robust cybersecurity defenses and a more resilient cyber ecosystem. Additionally, information sharing can help organizations comply with regulatory requirements and industry standards related to cybersecurity. Many regulatory frameworks, such as the General Data Protection Regulation (GDPR) and the Health Insurance Portability and Accountability Act (HIPAA), require organizations to implement measures to protect sensitive data and mitigate cybersecurity risks. By participating in information-sharing initiatives and adopting best practices recommended by industry groups, organizations can demonstrate due diligence and compliance with regulatory requirements, thereby reducing the risk of regulatory penalties and legal liabilities. Moreover, information sharing can play a crucial role in incident response and recovery efforts. In the event of a cybersecurity incident or data breach, timely and accurate information sharing can enable affected organizations to quickly identify the scope and severity of the attack, assess the impact on their systems and data, and coordinate an effective response with other stakeholders. By sharing threat intelligence data, indicators of compromise (IOCs), and other relevant information with incident response teams, law enforcement agencies, and cybersecurity vendors, organizations can expedite the investigation process, contain the damage, and restore normal operations more efficiently. Additionally, information sharing can help organizations build stronger relationships with customers, partners, and stakeholders by demonstrating a commitment to transparency, collaboration, and shared responsibility for cybersecurity. By sharing information about their cybersecurity practices, risk management processes, and incident response capabilities, organizations can enhance trust and credibility with customers and partners, fostering stronger business relationships and reducing the potential impact of cyber incidents on their reputation and brand image. In summary, information sharing is essential for organizations to effectively defend against cyber threats, collaborate with industry peers, and enhance overall cybersecurity resilience. By exchanging threat intelligence data, best practices, and lessons learned with other organizations, cybersecurity professionals can gain valuable insights, resources, and support to strengthen their defenses, respond more effectively to cyber incidents, and build a more resilient cyber ecosystem.

Chapter 8: Legal and Ethical Considerations in Penetration Testing

Legal frameworks and compliance standards play a crucial role in shaping the landscape of cybersecurity, guiding organizations in their efforts to protect sensitive data, mitigate cyber risks, and maintain regulatory compliance. One of the primary legal frameworks that govern cybersecurity practices is the General Data Protection Regulation (GDPR), which was implemented by the European Union (EU) to strengthen data protection and privacy for individuals within the EU and the European Economic Area (EEA). The GDPR imposes strict requirements on organizations that process personal data, including requirements for obtaining consent, implementing data protection measures, and notifying individuals in the event of a data breach. Failure to comply with the GDPR can result in severe penalties, including fines of up to €20 million or 4% of global annual turnover, whichever is higher. Another significant legal framework is the Health Insurance Portability and Accountability Act (HIPAA), which regulates the handling of protected health information (PHI) in the United States. HIPAA establishes standards for the security and privacy of PHI, requiring covered entities and their business associates to implement safeguards to protect the confidentiality, integrity, and availability of PHI. Non-compliance with HIPAA can result in civil and criminal penalties, including fines of up to $1.5 million per violation. Additionally, the Payment Card Industry Data Security Standard (PCI DSS) is a set of security standards designed to protect payment card data and prevent credit card fraud. PCI DSS applies to organizations that handle payment card transactions, requiring them to implement security controls such as encryption, access control, and regular vulnerability assessments. Failure to comply with PCI DSS can result in financial penalties, increased transaction fees, and restrictions on the ability to process payment card transactions. Beyond these specific regulations, many industries have their own compliance standards and regulatory requirements related to cybersecurity. For example, the financial services sector is subject to regulations such as the Sarbanes-Oxley Act (SOX) and the Federal Financial Institutions Examination Council (FFIEC) guidelines, which mandate controls and reporting requirements to protect financial data and prevent fraud. Similarly, the healthcare industry must comply with regulations such as the Health Information Technology for Economic and Clinical Health (HITECH) Act and the Health Information Exchange (HIE) requirements, which govern the use and exchange of electronic health records (EHRs) and patient information. Moreover, government agencies and contractors are often subject to cybersecurity regulations such as the Federal Information Security Management Act (FISMA) and the National Institute of Standards and Technology (NIST) Cybersecurity Framework, which establish standards and best practices for securing federal information systems and data. Compliance with these regulations typically involves conducting risk assessments, implementing security controls, and maintaining documentation to demonstrate adherence to regulatory requirements. Furthermore, international standards such as ISO/IEC 27001 provide a framework for establishing, implementing, maintaining, and continually improving an information security management system (ISMS). ISO/IEC 27001 requires organizations to assess their security risks, implement appropriate controls, and undergo regular audits to achieve and maintain certification. Achieving compliance with these legal frameworks and standards requires a comprehensive approach to cybersecurity, encompassing policies, procedures, technologies, and training. Organizations must develop and implement security policies and procedures that align with regulatory requirements, establish security controls to protect sensitive data and systems, and provide ongoing training and awareness programs to educate employees about their roles and responsibilities in maintaining compliance. Additionally, organizations must regularly assess their cybersecurity posture, conduct risk assessments, and address any vulnerabilities or deficiencies identified through audits and assessments. By adhering to legal frameworks and compliance standards, organizations can enhance their cybersecurity resilience, protect sensitive data, and mitigate the risk of regulatory penalties and legal liabilities. Compliance with these regulations also helps build trust and credibility with customers, partners, and stakeholders, demonstrating a commitment to protecting privacy and safeguarding sensitive information. In summary, legal frameworks and compliance standards are essential components of cybersecurity governance, guiding organizations in their efforts to protect data, mitigate risks, and maintain regulatory compliance. By adhering to these regulations and standards, organizations can strengthen their cybersecurity posture, protect sensitive information, and reduce the risk of regulatory penalties and legal liabilities. Ethical guidelines for penetration testers are fundamental principles and standards that govern the conduct and behavior of individuals engaged in penetration testing activities, ensuring that they operate in an ethical, responsible, and lawful manner. These guidelines serve as a framework for maintaining integrity, professionalism, and respect for the rights and privacy of others throughout the penetration testing process. One of the primary ethical considerations for penetration testers is obtaining proper authorization before conducting any testing activities. This involves obtaining explicit permission from the organization or individual responsible for the systems or networks being tested, typically through a formal agreement or contract. Without proper authorization, penetration testing activities may be considered unauthorized access or hacking, potentially leading to legal consequences. Once authorization is obtained, penetration testers must adhere to the scope and rules of engagement established for the engagement. This includes respecting any limitations or restrictions imposed by the client, such as specific systems or applications that are off-limits for testing, as well as any constraints on the timing or duration of testing activities. Failure to comply with the agreed-upon scope can lead to misunderstandings, disruptions, or damage to the client's systems and reputation. Additionally, penetration testers must exercise caution and discretion when conducting testing activities to avoid causing harm or disruption to the organization's operations. This includes minimizing the impact on production systems, avoiding actions that could lead to data loss or corruption, and following best practices for safe and responsible testing. For example, testers should refrain from launching denial-of-service attacks or brute-force attacks that could overwhelm or disrupt critical systems or services. Furthermore, penetration testers must respect the confidentiality and privacy of sensitive information encountered during testing. This includes exercising discretion when handling sensitive data such as personally identifiable information (PII), financial records, or proprietary business information. Testers should only access and disclose information that is directly relevant to the objectives of the engagement and obtain proper authorization before accessing any confidential or restricted data. In addition to respecting the confidentiality of data, penetration testers must also protect the integrity and availability of systems and networks under test. This involves taking precautions to prevent accidental damage or disruption to systems, as well as implementing safeguards to minimize the risk of exploitation by malicious actors. For example, testers should ensure that they have appropriate backups in place before conducting any potentially destructive tests and take steps to restore systems to their original state after testing is complete. Moreover, penetration testers must maintain honesty and transparency in their communications with clients, stakeholders, and other parties involved in the testing process.

This includes providing accurate and timely reporting of findings, vulnerabilities, and recommendations, as well as disclosing any conflicts of interest or potential biases that may impact the objectivity of their assessments. Testers should also refrain from engaging in deceptive or misleading practices, such as falsifying test results or misrepresenting their credentials or qualifications. Additionally, penetration testers must continually update their skills and knowledge to stay abreast of emerging threats, vulnerabilities, and best practices in the field. This includes participating in professional development activities, obtaining relevant certifications, and seeking out opportunities for hands-on experience and mentorship. By continually enhancing their skills and expertise, testers can ensure that they are well-equipped to conduct thorough, effective, and ethical penetration testing engagements. In summary, ethical guidelines for penetration testers are essential principles and standards that govern the conduct and behavior of individuals engaged in penetration testing activities. By adhering to these guidelines, testers can uphold integrity, professionalism, and respect for the rights and privacy of others, while also ensuring the effectiveness and legality of their testing efforts.

Chapter 9: Building Secure Infrastructure from Scratch

Secure system design principles encompass a set of fundamental concepts and practices aimed at creating robust, resilient, and trustworthy software and hardware systems that can withstand various cyber threats and attacks. One of the key principles of secure system design is the principle of least privilege, which states that users, processes, and systems should only be granted the minimum level of access or permissions necessary to perform their intended functions. This helps minimize the potential impact of security breaches or compromises by limiting the ability of attackers to access sensitive data or execute malicious actions. Another essential principle is defense in depth, which involves implementing multiple layers of security controls and mechanisms to protect against different types of threats and vulnerabilities. This includes measures such as firewalls, intrusion detection systems, encryption, and access controls, which work together to create overlapping layers of defense that can mitigate the risk of successful attacks. Additionally, secure system design emphasizes the importance of secure by default configurations, which means that systems should be configured to operate securely out of the box, with minimal additional configuration or customization required. This helps reduce the likelihood of misconfigurations or oversights that could create security vulnerabilities or expose systems to exploitation. Moreover, secure system design incorporates the principle of fail-safe defaults, which means that systems should be designed to fail in a safe and secure manner when unexpected conditions or errors occur. This helps prevent catastrophic failures or security breaches that could result from system crashes, software bugs, or other unforeseen events. Furthermore, secure system design emphasizes the importance of input validation and sanitization, which involves validating and sanitizing all input data received by a system to prevent malicious input from causing security vulnerabilities such as buffer overflows, injection attacks, or command injection. This helps ensure that only valid, safe input is processed by the system, reducing the risk of exploitation by attackers. Additionally, secure system design includes the principle of secure communication, which involves encrypting data transmissions and implementing secure communication protocols such as SSL/TLS to protect the confidentiality, integrity, and authenticity of data exchanged between systems. This helps prevent eavesdropping, tampering, or interception of sensitive information by unauthorized parties. Moreover, secure system design emphasizes the importance of secure coding practices, which involves following established coding standards and best practices to minimize the risk of common programming errors and vulnerabilities such as buffer overflows, injection attacks, and integer overflows. This includes techniques such as input validation, proper error handling, and secure memory management, which help ensure that software is robust, reliable, and resistant to exploitation. Additionally, secure system design incorporates the principle of continuous monitoring and testing, which involves regularly monitoring system activity and performance, as well as conducting periodic security assessments and penetration tests to identify and remediate vulnerabilities and weaknesses. This helps ensure that systems remain secure over time and can adapt to evolving threats and attack techniques. Furthermore, secure system design emphasizes the importance of secure deployment and configuration management, which involves implementing secure deployment procedures and practices to ensure that systems are securely configured and maintained throughout their lifecycle. This includes measures such as patch management, software updates, and configuration audits, which help reduce the risk of security breaches and ensure that systems remain up-to-date and resilient to emerging threats. Moreover, secure system design incorporates the principle of secure data storage and disposal, which involves implementing secure data storage practices such as encryption, access controls, and data masking to protect sensitive information from unauthorized access or disclosure. Additionally, secure system design includes the principle of resilience and recoverability, which involves designing systems to be resilient to failures, disruptions, and attacks, and implementing robust backup and recovery procedures to ensure that systems can quickly recover from incidents and continue to operate effectively. This includes measures such as data backups, disaster recovery planning, and redundant infrastructure, which help minimize downtime and ensure business continuity in the event of a security breach or other adverse event. In summary, secure system design principles are essential guidelines and practices that help organizations create and maintain secure, resilient, and trustworthy systems that can withstand various cyber threats and attacks. By incorporating these principles into their design and development processes, organizations can reduce the risk of security breaches, protect sensitive information, and ensure the reliability and integrity of their systems and data. Implementing secure infrastructure involves a comprehensive approach to designing, deploying, and managing the underlying technology stack that supports an organization's IT operations. One of the foundational best practices for implementing secure infrastructure is to start with a thorough risk assessment and threat modeling process, which helps identify potential security risks, vulnerabilities, and threats that could impact the organization's infrastructure. This involves analyzing the organization's assets, network architecture, data flows, and business processes to identify potential weaknesses and prioritize security measures accordingly. Additionally, implementing secure infrastructure requires following the principle of least privilege, which involves granting users, processes, and systems only the minimum level of access or permissions necessary to perform their intended functions. This helps minimize the potential impact of security breaches or compromises by limiting the ability of attackers to access sensitive data or execute malicious actions. Furthermore, implementing secure infrastructure involves implementing strong access controls and authentication mechanisms to verify the identity of users and ensure that only authorized individuals have access to sensitive resources and information. This includes measures such as multi-factor authentication, role-based access controls, and privileged access management, which help prevent unauthorized access and mitigate the risk of insider threats. Moreover, implementing secure infrastructure requires implementing robust network security measures to protect against external threats and attacks. This includes measures such as firewalls, intrusion detection systems, and network segmentation, which help monitor and control the flow of traffic between different network segments and protect against unauthorized access and malicious activity. Additionally, implementing secure infrastructure involves encrypting sensitive data both in transit and at rest to protect against eavesdropping, interception, and unauthorized access. This includes using strong encryption algorithms and protocols such as SSL/TLS to secure communications between systems and encrypting data stored on servers, databases, and other storage devices to protect against data breaches and theft. Furthermore, implementing secure infrastructure requires implementing regular security updates and patches to address known vulnerabilities and weaknesses in software and hardware components. This includes keeping operating systems, applications, and firmware up-to-date with the latest security patches and updates released by vendors, as well as regularly scanning and testing infrastructure components for vulnerabilities and misconfigurations. Moreover, implementing secure infrastructure involves implementing robust incident response and disaster recovery procedures to quickly detect, respond to, and recover from security incidents and breaches. This includes establishing clear incident response roles and responsibilities, creating incident response playbooks and procedures, and regularly testing and exercising incident response plans to ensure they are effective and reliable. Additionally, implementing secure infrastructure requires implementing strong physical security measures to protect against unauthorized access, theft, and tampering of hardware and infrastructure components. This includes measures such as access controls, surveillance cameras, and alarm systems to monitor and control physical access to data centers, server rooms, and other critical infrastructure facilities. Furthermore, implementing secure infrastructure involves implementing comprehensive security monitoring and logging capabilities to detect and respond to security incidents and breaches in real-time. This includes deploying security information and event management (SIEM) systems, intrusion detection and prevention systems (IDPS), and endpoint detection and response (EDR) solutions to monitor and analyze network traffic, system logs, and user activity for signs of suspicious or malicious behavior. Moreover, implementing secure infrastructure requires implementing regular security awareness training and education programs to educate employees about security best practices, threats, and risks, and empower them to recognize and report suspicious activity or security incidents. This includes providing training on topics such as phishing awareness, password security, and social engineering techniques to help employees understand their role in maintaining a secure infrastructure environment. Additionally, implementing secure infrastructure involves conducting regular security audits and assessments to evaluate the effectiveness of security controls and identify areas for improvement. This includes conducting penetration tests, vulnerability assessments, and security audits to identify weaknesses and vulnerabilities in infrastructure components, as well as evaluating compliance with industry standards and regulatory requirements. Furthermore, implementing secure infrastructure requires establishing strong partnerships and collaboration with vendors, partners, and other stakeholders to share threat intelligence, best practices, and security information. This includes participating in industry forums, information-sharing groups, and collaborative initiatives to stay informed about emerging threats and trends, as well as collaborating with vendors and partners to address security issues and vulnerabilities in a timely manner. In summary, implementing secure infrastructure requires a holistic approach that encompasses people, processes, and technology to protect against a wide range of threats and vulnerabilities. By following best practices such as risk assessment, least privilege, access controls, network security, encryption, patch management, incident response, physical security, security monitoring, security awareness training, security audits, and collaboration with stakeholders, organizations can build and maintain a secure infrastructure environment that can withstand various cyber threats and attacks.

Chapter 10: Industry Best Practices and Case Studies

Real-world case studies in cybersecurity incidents provide invaluable insights into the evolving threat landscape, the impact of cyber attacks on organizations, and the effectiveness of incident response strategies. One notable case study is the WannaCry ransomware attack that occurred in May 2017, which affected hundreds of thousands of computers worldwide. The attack exploited a vulnerability in the Microsoft Windows operating system, known as EternalBlue, which was allegedly developed by the United States National Security Agency (NSA) and leaked by a hacker group called the Shadow Brokers. The ransomware spread rapidly across networks by exploiting the vulnerability and encrypting files on infected computers, demanding ransom payments in Bitcoin for their release. The WannaCry attack had a significant impact on organizations across various sectors, including healthcare, finance, and government, causing disruption to critical services and financial losses estimated in the billions of dollars. Another notable case study is the Equifax data breach that occurred in 2017, where cybercriminals exploited a vulnerability in the

Apache Struts web application framework to gain unauthorized access to sensitive data belonging to approximately 147 million individuals. The breach exposed a vast amount of personal information, including names, Social Security numbers, birth dates, addresses, and in some cases, driver's license numbers and credit card details. The incident resulted in widespread public outrage, regulatory scrutiny, and legal consequences for Equifax, including fines and settlements totaling hundreds of millions of dollars. Additionally, the NotPetya ransomware attack, which occurred in June 2017, targeted organizations primarily in Ukraine but quickly spread globally, affecting companies in various industries. NotPetya used the same EternalBlue exploit as WannaCry to propagate across networks but also incorporated other propagation methods, such as credential theft and remote administration tools. The attack caused widespread disruption to businesses and critical infrastructure, including transportation, energy, and telecommunications, with estimated damages exceeding billions of dollars. Furthermore, the SolarWinds supply chain attack, discovered in December 2020, involved sophisticated threat actors compromising the software build and distribution process of SolarWinds' Orion platform, a widely used IT management software. The attackers inserted a malicious backdoor into legitimate software updates, allowing them to gain unauthorized access to thousands of organizations worldwide, including government agencies, technology firms, and Fortune 500 companies. The incident highlighted the risks associated with software supply chain attacks and the importance of rigorous security measures throughout the software development lifecycle. Moreover, the Colonial Pipeline ransomware attack, which occurred in May 2021, disrupted the operations of one of the largest fuel pipelines in the United States, leading to fuel shortages and price spikes along the East Coast. The attack involved the DarkSide ransomware group gaining unauthorized access to Colonial Pipeline's IT systems and encrypting critical data, forcing the company to shut down pipeline operations to contain the breach. The incident underscored the vulnerability of critical infrastructure to cyber attacks and the potential consequences of disruptions to essential services. In summary, real-world case studies in cybersecurity incidents offer valuable lessons for organizations seeking to strengthen their security posture and mitigate the risks of cyber threats. By analyzing the tactics, techniques, and procedures employed by threat actors in notable incidents such as WannaCry, Equifax, NotPetya, SolarWinds, and Colonial Pipeline, organizations can better understand the evolving threat landscape and develop proactive measures to detect, prevent, and respond to cyber attacks effectively. Adopting industry best practices for cybersecurity defense is crucial for organizations to enhance their resilience against evolving cyber threats and safeguard sensitive data and critical assets. One fundamental best practice is to establish a robust cybersecurity framework based on recognized standards such as the NIST Cybersecurity Framework, ISO/IEC 27001, or the CIS Controls. These frameworks provide comprehensive guidelines and controls for implementing effective cybersecurity measures tailored to the organization's risk profile and compliance requirements. Implementing a robust access control policy is essential to prevent unauthorized access to sensitive systems and data. This includes enforcing the principle of least privilege, where users are granted only the minimum level of access required to perform their job functions, and implementing strong authentication mechanisms such as multi-factor authentication (MFA) to protect against credential theft and unauthorized access attempts. Regularly updating and patching software and systems is critical to address known vulnerabilities and reduce the risk of exploitation by threat actors. Organizations should establish a formal patch management process to identify, prioritize, and apply security patches in a timely manner, leveraging tools such as Windows Server Update Services (WSUS) or Red Hat Satellite for centralized patch deployment and management. Conducting regular vulnerability assessments and penetration testing is essential to identify and remediate security weaknesses before they can be exploited by attackers. Tools such as Nessus, OpenVAS, or Qualys can be used to scan networks and systems for known vulnerabilities, while penetration testing tools like Metasploit or Burp Suite can simulate real-world attack scenarios to assess the effectiveness of defensive controls. Implementing network segmentation and segregation controls can help mitigate the impact of a security breach by containing the spread of malware or unauthorized access within the network. This involves dividing the network into separate zones or segments and enforcing strict access controls between them, using techniques such as virtual LANs (VLANs), firewalls, and network access control (NAC) solutions. Deploying advanced endpoint protection solutions such as next-generation antivirus (NGAV), endpoint detection and response (EDR), and endpoint protection platforms (EPP) can help organizations detect and block sophisticated malware, ransomware, and other endpoint threats. Solutions like CrowdStrike Falcon, Carbon Black, or Microsoft Defender ATP leverage machine learning, behavioral analysis, and threat intelligence to identify and respond to malicious activities in real-time. Implementing robust encryption mechanisms for data in transit and at rest is essential to protect sensitive information from unauthorized access or interception. Organizations should use strong cryptographic algorithms and protocols such as Transport Layer Security (TLS) for securing network communications and encryption standards like AES or RSA for protecting data stored on servers, databases, or removable media. Educating employees about cybersecurity best practices and raising awareness about common threats such as phishing, social engineering, and ransomware is essential to create a security-aware culture within the organization. Conducting regular security awareness training sessions, phishing simulations, and providing resources such as posters, newsletters, and online courses can help employees recognize and respond to security threats effectively. Establishing an incident response plan and team is critical to enable organizations to respond swiftly and effectively to cybersecurity incidents when they occur. The incident response plan should outline procedures for detecting, analyzing, containing, and recovering from security breaches, as well as roles and responsibilities of incident response team members. Tools such as Security Information and Event Management (SIEM) platforms, log management systems, and incident response orchestration platforms can facilitate incident detection, analysis, and response activities by aggregating and correlating security event data from across the organization's IT infrastructure. Regularly reviewing and updating cybersecurity policies, procedures, and controls is essential to adapt to evolving threats and regulatory requirements. Organizations should conduct periodic security audits and assessments to evaluate the effectiveness of their cybersecurity program and identify areas for improvement. By continuously monitoring and improving their cybersecurity posture, organizations can better protect themselves against cyber threats and minimize the risk of data breaches, financial losses, and reputational damage.

Conclusion

In summary, the "PENTEST+ EXAM PASS: (PT0-002)" book bundle offers a comprehensive and structured approach to preparing cybersecurity professionals for the CompTIA PenTest+ certification exam. Across four books, this bundle covers foundational fundamentals, advanced techniques and tools, network exploitation and defense strategies, as well as expert insights and real-world scenarios.

Book 1 provides readers with a solid understanding of the foundational concepts and methodologies essential for penetration testing and vulnerability management. It lays the groundwork for more advanced topics covered in subsequent books.

Book 2 delves into advanced techniques and tools used by cybersecurity professionals to identify, exploit, and mitigate vulnerabilities in complex environments. It equips readers with practical skills and knowledge to tackle sophisticated cyber threats effectively.

Book 3 focuses on network exploitation and defense strategies, offering insights into the intricacies of network security and how attackers exploit vulnerabilities to compromise systems. It also provides valuable guidance on implementing defensive measures to protect against such attacks.

Book 4 takes readers beyond the exam syllabus, offering expert insights and real-world scenarios to deepen their understanding of penetration testing and vulnerability management. Through case studies and practical examples, readers gain valuable insights into the challenges and complexities of real-world cybersecurity scenarios.

Together, these books provide a comprehensive and practical resource for cybersecurity professionals seeking to pass the CompTIA PenTest+ exam and advance their careers in the field. Whether you are a novice looking to build a strong foundation or an experienced practitioner seeking to enhance your skills, the "PENTEST+ EXAM PASS: (PT0-002)" book bundle offers valuable insights and guidance to help you succeed in the dynamic and challenging field of cybersecurity.